Frames
and ◆
Framing

The Ultimate Illustrated
How-to-Do-It Guide

Dedication

To Terry Laird and Paxton Dunn
for their patience . . .

. . . and to Joan Scholtes
for her hard work and well-spent time.

No. 2909
$19.95

Frames
and
Framing

The Ultimate Illustrated How-to-Do-It Guide

Gerald F. Laird and
Louise Meière Dunn, CPF

TAB BOOKS Inc.

Blue Ridge Summit, PA

Notices

Alto EZ Mat is a registered trademark of Alto Company.
Color Mount and Seal are registered trademarks of Seal Corporation.
Dax is a registered trademark of Dax Manufacturing, Inc.
Denglas is a trademark of Denton Vacuum Inc.
Dexter Mat Cutter is a registered trademark of Dexter.
Elmer's is a registered trademark of Bordon.
Elpa is a registered trademark of Elpa.
Filmoplast SH and Filmoplast P-90 are registered trademarks of Neschen International.
Framespace is a trademark of Frametek.
Fletcher is a registered trademark of Fletcher-Terry Co.
Innerspace is a trademark of Buckwalter.
Insta-Hinge is a registered trademark of Archival Products.
Liquid Leaf and Treasure Gold are registered trademarks of Plaid Enterprises.
Logan is a registered trademark of Logan Corp.
Masonite is a trademark of Masonite Corporation.
Mighty Mounts is a registered trademark of R&D Framing Co.
Plexiglas is a trademark of Rohm & Hass Co.
Rub 'n Buff is a trademark of American Art Clay Co., Inc.
Scotch and C&H Mat Cutter are registered trademarks of 3M Co.
Sobo is a registered trademark of The Slomons Group.
Uni-Frame 40 is a trademark of Elibank Frame Inc.
Woolite is a trademark of Proctor & Gamble.
X-Acto is a registered trademark of X-ACTO.

FIRST EDITION
FIRST PRINTING

Copyright © 1988 by TAB BOOKS Inc.
Printed in the United States of America

Library of Congress Cataloging in Publication Data

Laird, Gerald F.
    Frames and framing.

    Includes index.
    1. Picture frames and framing. I. Dunn, Louise
Meiere. II. Title.
N8550.L25 1987   749'.7   87-18009
ISBN 0-8306-0309-3
ISBN 0-8306-2909-2 (pbk.)

Questions regarding the content of this book should be addressed to:

    Reader Inquiry Branch
    TAB BOOKS Inc.
    Blue Ridge Summit, PA 17294-0214

    TAB would like to thank Dan and Becky Dietrich of A Little Gallery, Mont Alto, Pennsylvania, for kindly allowing the use of their gallery and equipment for photographing the cover and parts of the color section.

Contents

PREFACE

The information in this book was obtained from many sources and double-checked for reliability. All suggestions are based on expert guidance. The projects were done, all or in part, by the authors. Because words can be interpreted differently, however, we suggest that you practice all methods and procedures on inexpensive materials before trying them on more expensive projects. We emphasize this point throughout the book. With practice, you will be able to do any of the projects, but please don't take an expensive piece of silk and start making a covered mat by just following our directions. You must practice using materials from your scrap collections. TAB BOOKS Inc. and the authors disclaim all responsibility for loss or damage that might happen from using information found in this book.

ACKNOWLEDGMENTS

For their help and contributions in preparing this book, we thank Paul Scholtes; Kitty Sample; Donna Shuford; Joan and Charles Heston; Bob Allen; D.J. and Edgar Geibel; Richard Kluga; John Kupik; Phil Philippas, Hilly Kupik, and Greg Mayers of the Camera Shops in Stamford; Greg Fremster of Frametek; Bob Sylvester of the Fletcher-Terry Company; and Suzanne Perkins, D'Arcy Deeves, and Jerome Golenbock of Regency Galleries of Stamford.

INTRODUCTION

You can master the art of framing.

This comprehensive how-to-do-it book provides illustrated step-by-step procedures so the beginner can construct frames for watercolors, prints, diplomas, bark paintings, photographs, oils, fans, needlepoint, shadow boxes, rubbings, and posters. You will be shown, step by step, many procedures, from cutting mats to selecting the hardware and wire for hanging your completed frames.

You already have all the skills you need. All the information is here to set them in action. You will need a few basic tools, and you probably own some of them already. It doesn't matter if you are a fast or slow worker. With a little imagination and patience, together with the basic steps that are discussed in depth here, you will be able to frame artwork that will look as if it had been done by a professional. It could open doors to a whole new world for you.

TO ERR IS HUMAN

It seems only fair to warn you that even the most experienced framer makes a mistake now and then, and it is frustrating when you are that framer. Do not despair! Tips on how to anticipate and avoid the most likely mistakes are provided, and tricks for recovering from the mistakes you do make are suggested. These will be highlighted as follows:

☞ In cutting wood for a frame, always cut the long sides first. If you goof and cut it too short, you can use it as one of your short sides.

Once you complete your first frame, you will experience a tremendous feeling of satisfaction. You will reach that high quicker if you pay careful attention to what you are doing and are very careful with your measurements. Unfortunately, it is easy to cut a 45-degree angle in the wrong direction when you are not thinking about how it will look as part of a completed frame. The corner angle always points into the art. It is embarrassing to have the edges that are meant to hold the artwork all pointing outward. So, before you make that first cut, go back and check your measurements. Visualize the completed frame, verify your marks, then cut. If you feel at all unsure, go back and do it one more time. Hang in there. You'll get it. Once you do, you'll be ecstatic.

PRACTICE MAKES PERFECT FRAMES

In learning the basics of any subject, repetition pays off. Practice cutting mats and moldings on expendable material before you cut into anything that you are considering for use in the finished frame. Do not cut into fabric that you have bought for use as a finished insert or liner cover until you have read the chapter on how to do it and have tried your skill on scraps.

Read how to do it first, test the skills you have learned, and then test them again. This method will pay off in a better product. There is a certain knack to each step, which you will acquire with a little practice. You will be amazed at how easy it all seems after you have had just a little practice.

Remember, a frame is meant to enhance, support, and protect the artwork. It should not call attention to itself.

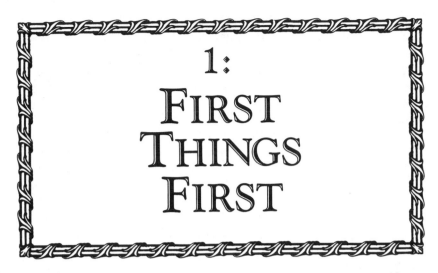

1:
FIRST
THINGS
FIRST

If you have never cut a frame or mat before, and perhaps even if you have, there are things you need to review before you pick up a saw or mat cutter. Because the various steps in framing are so interrelated, you must know everything you plan to do before you actually do anything. Do not read about how to cut a frame and then dash out and cut a frame before you have considered all the other elements that will go into the creation of the entire package.

Read through the information on tools, terms, and the basic steps, as well as one or two of the projects in this book, before you attempt to make your first frame. In this way you can avoid making expensive mistakes, which happen when you fail to think out the entire project in advance.

SETTING UP YOUR WORK AREA

Never underestimate the importance of a proper work space. Most people do not have a fully equipped shop available, but you need at least a sturdy, stable, and perfectly flat working area. Otherwise, you will end up with irregular cuts and ruined mat boards. Do not attempt to work on a shaky card table in a corner of your living room or use one of those folding aluminum tables that have a tendency to fold at crucial times.

SELECTING BASIC AND OPTIONAL TOOLS

When it comes to expenditures, buy the best tools and materials that your present circumstances can afford. The frustrations in learning the art of framing often stem from trying to cope with inadequate or inexpensive equipment or make-do materials.

Each operation in framing calls for basic tools. Like everything else in life, economics rears its ugly head. Unfortunately, the better and, it often seems, easier to use tools cost more. It is possible, however, to do wonders with the following tools: a sharp pencil, corner clamps, a miter box and backsaw, a small drill or awl, a T square, a 2- or 3-foot steel-edged ruler, a mat cutter (for windows), a utility knife (for outside edges of mats), a glass cutter, a razor blade, hardware (screw eyes, wire hangers, wire), a screwdriver, pliers, a hammer and nails (brads), wood glue, and white glue.

There are other specific tools that can make your framing work easier. In the step-by-step discussions of each project, these alternative items will be shown and discussed. You can decide whether the economics of your operation warrant the cost or convenience. With these basic tools, you can do the projects in this book. Before buying any tools, read through the projects and study the optional tools we use. Consider carefully before you make any specific purchases. If you know right now that you will be making a lot of frames or cutting mats in quantity, do not waste money on cheaper, interim tools. The better tool can make the job go faster because it will help you achieve a greater level of accuracy sooner. Invest in quality tools in the beginning, after considering your options.

Try to take into account what your immediate and future needs will be, although it is impossible to predict the utility of every item for every framer. Only after you have been working with the basic tools will you be able to decide what you need to "step up" your equipment. These items do not call for a big outlay of money and should pay for themselves in a relatively short time. If you decide later that you need an air hammer or a dry-mount press, the basic equipment you buy now will have been amortized. Besides, you can always use an extra hammer around the house.

Miter Box and Backsaw

To make a perfect frame, you must have perfectly mitered corners. In cutting the 45-degree angles for your mitered corners, you must have absolute accuracy. If you do not, you will not get square corners. Without square corners, you will have trouble with your glass, your mat boards, and everything else that follows.

The only way to cut these angles, without using professional equipment, is with a miter box and backsaw. Some say it is easy to make your own miter box. Wrong! It is not a very efficient use of time or talent when you can buy a better one for a few dollars. Any miter box will only be accurate if the guides are accurate and you use it carefully. The angle guides in the cheaper wooden miter boxes tend to wear rapidly and will start to cut angles that are not true.

There are problems in using a cheap miter box to cut your first frame. You could become discouraged very early if you cut a frame and then discover that the angles are off, although you did everything you were told to do. You should start with a hardwood or plastic miter box and cut your first frames with care and patience. If you find you like framing, you can graduate to a semiprofessional rig, or even a professional cutter later.

For most of the projects in this book, we used the Stanley unit shown in Fig. 1-1, and found it to be an excellent investment. First, however, we used several smaller miter boxes made of hard oak, plastic, and metal (Figs. 1-2 to 1-4). We continued to use these when it was not convenient to keep the larger one set up and ready for operation.

You must clamp or fasten the miter box permanently to your work area to hold it firmly. You also need a piece of scrap wood on the floor of your miter box. To cut framing molding, you must make a clean cut all the way through the molding, and the scrap wood prevents the saw blade from coming in contact with the metal, wood, or plastic base. If you don't cut all the way through, you end up with a feathered edge that is virtually impossible to join properly in the corner clamp or miter vise when you are forming your mitered corners. You might be able to sand down a slightly feathered edge with an emery board or very fine sandpaper, however.

A framer's saw or backsaw has a built in spine down the back to hold it more rigidly than the ordinary saws. It must have a thin, firm blade with no nicks in the saw teeth for cutting accuracy.

☞ If your saw feels loose in the miter box, put a strip of plastic tape down the length of the saw on both sides (Fig. 1-5) to hold it tighter in the guide.

In sawing, the weight of the saw itself does the cutting. You should use long, steady strokes with little or no exertion of your own. Never use short, jerky, back-and-forth strokes. They make the saw flare out more, widening your cut. This motion also tends to make the saw flip out of the miter box, creating an uneven cut that might be unusable. Do not push or force the saw.

You can use a pressure clamp to hold the wood in position in the miter box when holding it with your free hand will not keep it steady enough. The wood should be immobile while cutting. Be careful that the pressure from the clamp does not lift the wood off the floor of your miter box, though, or you will get a distorted cut. Also be careful that it does not press into soft woods and make a dent on the surface which will show on the finished frame. From a safety standpoint, while you are holding the wood, be careful that you do not place your hand too close to the saw blade.

Corner Clamps and a Miter Vise

You can get by with one corner clamp, but it is slow going. You really need four. Yes, you can form your corner, glue and nail it, and then let it set in one clamp until it is firm enough to remove the clamp.

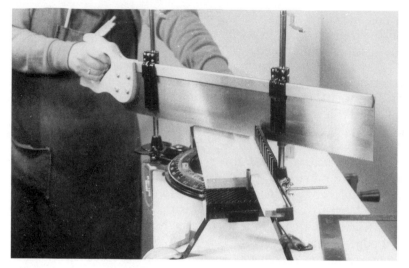

Fig. 1-1. *Stanley Mitre Box (Model 19-160). Note that it is firmly clamped to the workbench. This is the miter box used for most of the work done in this book.*

Fig. 1-2. *Basic hardwood miter box. Note spring clamp holding wood.*

Fig. 1-3. *Hard plastic miter box.*

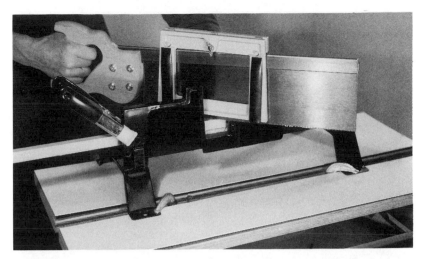

Fig. 1-4. *Metal miter box with free floating saw guide and built-in angle guides.*

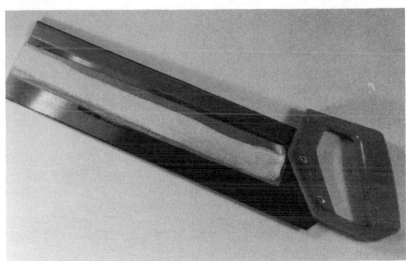

Fig. 1-5. *A strip of tape placed on both sides of the saw blade can help hold it more firmly in case the grooves of your wood miter box should widen with use.*

It is better, however, to have enough clamps so you don't waste time. Leave that first corner in its clamp, use another one to form the opposite corner, then two more to finish the frame (Fig. 1-6).

The miter vise (Fig. 1-7) is the first of the "buy-it-if-you-can-afford-it" tools (meaning it is not absolutely essential, but it is a very desirable convenience). This excellent tool acts as an extra hand that holds the corner perfectly clamped while you line up the miters. It then holds the corner perfectly in place while you apply glue or decide where the brads will go. Both hands are free to predrill, if necessary, or just to hammer in the brads. It is also more convenient when you use your nail set.

You can clamp a corner clamp to your workbench in place of a miter vise, but it is not nearly as maneuverable, convenient, or satisfactory as doing your initial corner work with a miter vise. With a miter vise,

Fig. 1-6. *Corner clamps hold the four sides of a frame in position while the glue in mitered corners is drying.*

Fig. 1-7. *A miter vise holds the frame in position for final corner assembly. Note the wood blocks holding the frame level with the miter vise.*

Fig. 1-8. *Adjustable picture framing clamps. There are extra rods and adapter nuts for larger frames.*

you have the convenience of using different types of corner clamping systems (Figs. 1-8 and 1-9). This is important if you are doing more than one job at a time or are working with frames that might need a firmer clamp (Fig. 1-10).

It is possible to use a regular workbench vise to join corners, but it is difficult at best and not recommended. You will not have the freedom a miter vise gives you, by allowing you to adjust the corners perfectly before you add the glue and nail the corner.

Hammer and Brads

You probably have a hammer, but chances are you do not have an upholsterer's hammer or a tack hammer (Fig. 1-11), which is what you need to make the job easier. These hammers have small heads and can hit nails without damaging the curved wood surfaces you often encounter in framing. Hammers with larger heads will make dents in the wood, no matter how careful you are. The size of the brad (*brads* are thin, tapered nails with almost no heads) will depend upon the depth you need to drive it and the width of wood you have available. If you are doing a variety of framing jobs, you will need an assortment of brads, starting with ½ inch, and working up to 1½ inches, or possibly more, depending on the size or depth of the wood you are nailing. Use a corrugated mitering nail (Fig. 1-12) if you are working with 4-inch or larger wood.

Nail Set

To prepare your frame for proper finishing, you need to push the brad deeper than your hammer can reach. You can use a nail set for this purpose (Fig. 1-11). Position the nail set over the nail you have just pounded in and tap it with your hammer twice: once to set up vibrations and once to drive it home. There will be a slight recession that you should fill with nail-hole filler, wood dough, or other special filling material, which is available in a variety of colors. The nail set keeps the nail from showing, as well as from rusting later and discoloring the finish.

Small Drill or Awl

More often than not when you are in framing, you will be dealing with thin strips of wood that require nails. If you use a small drill (Fig. 1-13) before you insert the nail, you can reduce the chances of splitting the wood. Make certain the hole you drill is smaller than the nail size you will be using to hold the frame together, or it won't hold.

Rulers, Straightedges, and Squares

Depending upon the size work you are doing, you need a steel ruler 2 or 3 feet long. It can double as a measuring device for many operations

Fig. 1-9. *(top left) An adjustable clamp holds the parting strip for a needlework project while the glue sets.*

Fig. 1-10. *(top right) A clip-type spring clamp can be used when extra pressure is required. It is especially useful while working with deep frames that corner clamps can't hold.*

Fig. 1-11. *Tack hammer. This type is best for most framing operations; it is shown here with a nail set.*

Fig. 1-12. *Corrugated mitering nail.*

and as a straightedge for mat or glass cutting. You might prefer to use a folding rule or a roll-in tape, but you still need a straightedge for cutting glass and mats.

A metal square is essential in checking your work for accurate 90-degree corners. After you have made your frame, check it before you cut your mats. If the frame is off, chances are the glass or mat will not fit. If it is only off a little, cut the mats and glass to the shorter of the two dimensions that do not match. If the frame is ¼ inch larger than you had planned, you must take the frame apart and cut it down to fit. If it is smaller, your artwork is not going to fit, and you must set this frame aside and make a new one. In many cases, however, you have a little leeway and can reduce the size of the mat, as long as it does not disturb the balance you are trying to achieve in displaying the artwork.

It is decisions such as these that make it unwise to cut your mat, backboards, or glass until you have completed your frame. Otherwise, if you make a slight mistake, you will definitely need to make a new frame in order to use your precut mats and glass.

Cutting Tools

Several basic mat cutters (Fig. 1-14) will be shown in the step-by-step projects. A professional cutter (Fig. 1-15) also will be discussed. The utility knife shown with the cutters in Fig. 1-14 is essential for cutting outside edges of mats and backing boards.

Sometimes a mat cutter leaves an infinitesimal section uncut. You can complete this cut with a razor blade. Do not try to complete these small cuts by inserting the mat cutter again. You probably will wreck your work. By carefully using a razor blade, you can complete the cut perfectly. With a little practice, you will make your beveled cuts without making overcuts on the front of the mat. While you are first learning, it is good to know that you can complete the last ¹⁄₁₆ inch with a razor blade. A razor blade is also very useful for cutting fabric-covered mats and inserts.

Glass Cutters

There are several types of glass cutters (Fig. 1-16). The least expensive ones are easy enough to master but should be kept in kerosene or oil when not in use, which might be considered a nuisance. A slightly more expensive diamond cutter needs no solution for storage, seems to be easier to use, and is recommended, especially if you have never cut glass before. Fletcher makes a self-lubricating glass cutter that has an additional swivel position for cutting curves, as well as a locked position for making straight cuts.

Gluing

When you are joining a frame together, make sure you use enough glue so it will become absorbed into the fiber of the wood. Dab it on

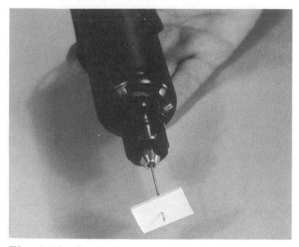

Fig. 1-13. *Small electric drill.*

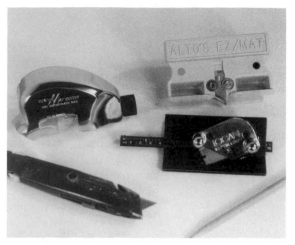

Fig. 1-14. *Hand-held mat cutters. Clockwise, upper right: Alto's EZ/Mat, the Logan, a utility knife, and the Dexter Cutter.*

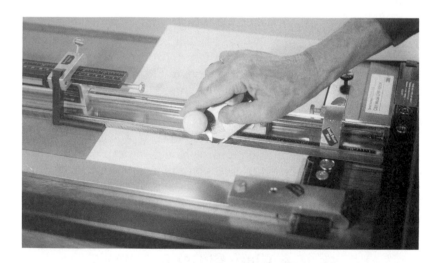

Fig. 1-15. *A professional mat cutter.*

Fig. 1-16. *Glass cutters. Top to bottom: the basic rotary blade type, a diamond tip, and a self-lubricating cutter.*

with your finger, a piece of scrap mat board, or the end of the glue dispenser. Be sure to spread it evenly over both pieces of wood. A hairline of glue should seep up when you squeeze the mitered corners together with corner clamps or a miter vise. Wipe off this excess glue right away, using a slightly moistened sponge or paper towel. For frames, a wood glue is recommended.

Screw Eyes, Wire, and Wall Hangers

Screw eyes and braided wire are generally used on the backs of frames. Both are available in various sizes, and the commercial packages indicate how much weight the hardware will support. There are also sawtooth hangers, mirror hangers, turnbuckles, and other hardware, which will be shown and discussed with specific projects.

Picture hangers are available in various weights. Weigh your finished frame (frame + glass + artwork + fillers); it is probably not as heavy as you might guess. If in doubt, be sure to use the heavier estimate or use two hangers and distribute the weight.

COMING TO TERMS

Although there is a Glossary in the back of this book, you should be familiar with the following terms before learning about framing materials. Remember, you need all the information before you can begin to understand the basic elements that make up the whole project. Each of these terms is discussed in detail in later "how-to" projects, and the Glossary gives you a concise definition. The terms discussed here are meant to help you grasp the various how-to steps before you cut your first piece of framing wood (molding) or mat board.

Molding. The basic outside of the frame. Although the term could be construed to be metal or plastic, it generally refers to wood used to produce a wooden frame. Framers are interested in two types: builder's molding (Fig. 1-17) and framer's molding (Fig. 1-18). *Framer's molding* is constructed with its own rabbet (see next definition). *Builder's molding* is wood that is specifically designed to be used for door sills, chair rails around rooms, cabinet shelving holders, and other decorative carpentry in home construction. Although it is decorative, it needs to have a rabbet to be suitable for use in framing. Do-it-yourself picture framers have learned to use various combinations of builder's molding to construct simple, as well as very dramatic, frame designs, adding some form of parting strip to the back to form the rabbet.

Caution! Be careful not to get carried away and combine so many different types of molding that it looks too complicated or too junky. Also, you might spend so much on a variety of builder's molding that it would have been less expensive and possibly more elegant to have picked out one from a professional framer. Done with taste, how-

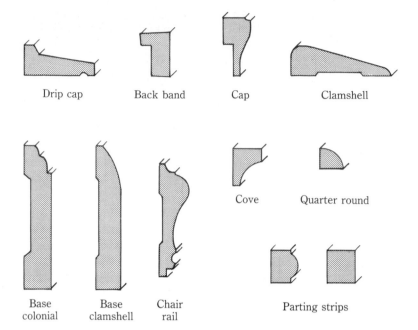

Drip cap   Back band   Cap   Clamshell

Cove   Quarter round

Base colonial   Base clamshell   Chair rail   Parting strips

Fig. 1-17. *Builder's molding.*

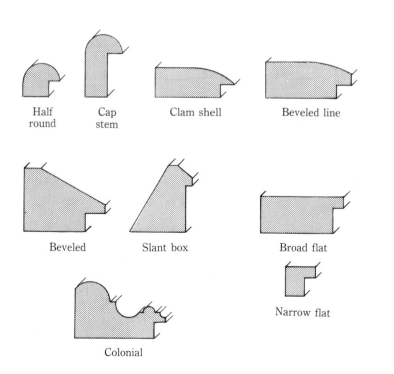

Half round   Cap stem   Clam shell   Beveled line

Beveled   Slant box   Broad flat

Narrow flat

Colonial

Fig. 1-18. *Framer's molding.*

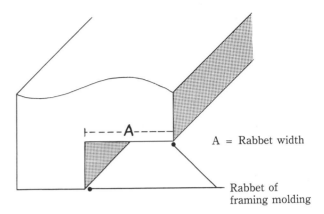

A = Rabbet width

Rabbet of framing molding

Fig. 1-19. *A rabbet; the right-angled notch under the frame.*

ever, builder's molding has a definite place in your operation. You will also take pride in creating your own frame.

Rabbet. The right angle notched out of the inner side of a frame (Fig. 1-19) and designed to hold the contents of the frame. It must be deep enough to contain artwork, mats, backing materials, and (if used) glass or glazing. (Oils and some fabrics often do not use glazing.)

Mat. Material (mat board, fabric-wrapped board, or wood) that keeps artwork from touching the glass while enhancing the artistic framing of the print, photograph, or other artwork. You can use more than one mat. The air space between artwork and glass provided by the mat(s) helps to eliminate the problems of moisture, image transfer, and mold and other fungus forms.

Liner. One of at least two different types of decorative devices that set off artwork. One, it is that piece of molding, sometimes wrapped with fabric, that separates an oil painting from its frame, sometimes called an *insert.* Two, it is the inner mat or mats when multiple mats are used around artwork.

Fillet. A form of liner or insert. It is a very thin strip that generally fits between the artwork and the frame; or it can be a delineation between two mats. It is usually gold (for warmth) or silver (for a cool look), and lends a formal or antique look to artwork.

Backboard or Substrate. The mat board that supports and holds the artwork in position. Sometimes the artwork is mounted to it with hinges or adhesive. The two terms are interchangeable. Some refer to it as a *mounting board.*

Backing or Filler Board. Again, two terms with but one meaning. The filler board is placed behind the backboard (and consequently, behind all the other elements in the frame, except for the dust cover) to hold it all in place. Depending upon the depth of the frame, you can use one or more filler boards. If you have a variety of foam-core board on hand, you can pick out the size you need to fill in the area from the backboard to the frame. Be sure to leave enough room to place the brads. If you do not have foam core, use whatever you have on hand. If you are concerned about conservation, do not use regular corrugated board. Use a corrugated board made to conservation standards.

Foam Core Board. Versatile, lightweight board consisting of two sheets of paper with various thicknesses of aerated plastic sandwiched between them. Depending upon quality and thickness, it can be used for filler or backboard or as an integral part of special frames.

Dust Cover. Kraft paper glued to the back of the frame before the hanging hardware is added. It keeps out dust, dirt, insects, and other foreign matter. It is sometimes reinforced with tape, although this step is not essential.

Framing Hardware. The screw eyes, wire, and hangers that are placed on the backs of frames, and their counterparts that are sunk or nailed into walls to hold and display artwork in a more or less permanent position.

2:

MAKING FRAMES

Once you have read this chapter, including the first projects that show you how to frame specific items, you will be ready to make your first frame. With this information and adequate practice (please take the time to practice), you will be able to create your own designs. The instructions here apply to almost any variation of frame.

CREATING A FRAME WITH BUILDER'S MOLDING

Using builder's molding for picture frames is very popular, probably stemming from the fact that it is almost impossible to buy picture-framing molding. If you can find it, it is more expensive than creating your own frames with builder's molding.

To create a frame using builder's molding, first choose your wood. Check through your local sources to see what's available. When you see a style that appeals to you, imagine how it will look as a frame. Visualize it alone or in combination with other moldings.

Unless you are very knowledgeable about woods, you should place yourself at the mercy of the people at your local lumberyard. In most cases, they will be very helpful and actually enjoy discussing your projects and sharing their knowledge. Remember that builder's molding becomes part of the overall construction of a building, and quality will vary. Here are a few things to check before you accept any strip of wood that the lumber dealer hands you:

1. Ask if it is kiln dried. Kiln-dried wood is preferred because it is less likely to shrink or warp.

2. Check for existing warping. Hold the wood in front of you and sight down the length.

3. Don't accept wood with knots, gouges, or other natural or man-made flaws. Pay special attention to the surface that will be the face of the frame.

4. Once you get it home, store the wood carefully to reduce the chances of warping. Lay it flat in a dry area. Don't stand it on end, unless you are desperate for space.

5. Check for consistent grain markings if you are going to wax or stain the finish. If you are planning to paint it with an opaque substance, this is not a problem.

Some lumberyards will rout out a rabbet for you. Although this is not a universal practice, it is worth checking. Learn a little more about what you are doing, however, before you go to your lumberyard and ask them to rout out a piece of wood that is already too thin to take a rabbet notch. Even with the thicker types of builder's molding, you should know how much of a rabbet you need. If you are using more than one mat or a foam core between mats, you will need a deeper rabbet than if you are making a very basic frame.

Some builder's molding is notched for a specific use, such as for cabinet shelving or screen doors. Some corner molding has a design that you can adapt to holding the framing package, without adding a parting strip. Most will need the parting strip. A few samples of builder's molding were shown in Fig. 1-17. You should see what's available at your local outlets. Each part of the country and every yard probably has a different type of stock.

For your first frames, stick to simple combinations of builder's molding that fit flat in your miter box. Molding designed for crowns, some coved woods, and larger sizes are difficult to handle at first. You also need some practice material. Make some corner samples to give you experience in using both the miter box and corner clamps. Since you probably do not have scraps of builder's molding, check your lumberyard. Many of them have an odds-and-ends barrel of remainders.

The usual method of using builder's molding is to add a parting strip to the molding to form a rabbet. Parting strips are available in various thicknesses. The ½-×-¾-inch strip is probably used most, but if you have a thin package in the frame, you can use a ½-×-½-inch strip. Once you start making your own frames, you will learn that various types of wood can be used to make a parting strip.

DETERMINING YOUR FRAMING REQUIREMENTS

One reason you should not cut a frame at this point is that you must learn how to determine the exact size of the frame. You need to know how wide the mat will be, if you are using one or more mats, how the picture or artwork will be mounted, and other basic information that will come later in this chapter. As a beginner, you are better off cutting and completing your frame first, then cutting your backboard, mats, and glass. If you make a slight mistake and end up with a frame

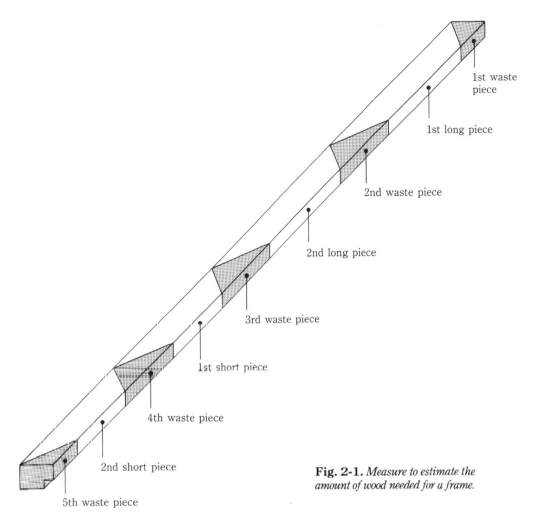

1st waste
piece

1st long piece

2nd waste piece

2nd long piece

3rd waste piece

1st short piece

4th waste piece

2nd short piece

5th waste piece

Fig. 2-1. *Measure to estimate the amount of wood needed for a frame.*

that is slightly larger or smaller than you intended, you probably can adapt the mats and glass to accommodate this mistake, and no one will ever know. If you already have cut the mats and glass, you either will need to cut new ones or cut a new frame. No one will ever know this, either, but it is a little more costly to you.

There is a formula to show you how to estimate the amount of wood you will need to build a frame. Look at Figs. 2-1 and 2-2 while reading the formula. They will help you visualize it. Figure 2-1 shows you the way you cut each side. Figure 2-2 shows exactly why you must use a piece the width of the molding on both ends of the wood to form a perfectly mitered corner. This is not the way you cut each side, but it will help you see what you are doing.

Assume you have chosen your artwork and potential mat size, and have decided to make a frame that will be 11 × 14 inches. This

Dotted lines are sawing lines.

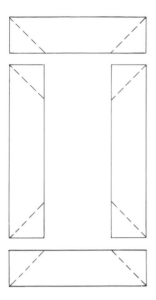
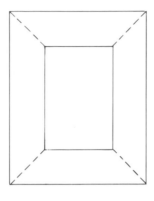

Fig. 2-2. *The waste wood that occurs when you miter the four corners of a frame.*

is your desired window measurement. The builder's molding width is 2 inches wide.

1. Add the four sides: 11 inches + 11 inches + 14 inches + 14 inches = 50 inches.

2. To figure waste wood, multiply 8 times the width of the molding. (See both illustrations but especially Fig. 2-2.) The molding is 2 inches wide: 8 × 2 inches = 16 inches.

3. To compensate for wood displaced by your saw while you are cutting the eight mitered corners, estimate ⅛ inch per saw cut, or a total of 1 inch. This is a constant figure to add to any wood frame you are cutting, whether you are using builder's or framer's molding.

4. Therefore, add the four sides, plus the waste wood, plus the sawdust displacement to get the amount of wood you need to make a frame. That is: 50 inches + 16 inches + 1 inch = 67 inches.

Most builder's molding is sold by the foot. Assuming you can buy perfect wood (wood without any flaws) and that you will make no mistakes, you can make an 11- × -14-inch frame with 6 feet of either framer's or builder's molding. Check to see what the policy is at the craft shops, hardware stores, and lumberyards in your locality. Perhaps you'll be lucky and find an inexpensive lumberyard that handles framer's molding. In any case, be sure to check for flaws before you accept any molding.

OTHER CONSIDERATIONS
IN CHOOSING A MOLDING

The design of your frame should relate to the artwork. This does not mean that simple artwork calls for simple frames. It could be just the opposite.

It also should relate to the matting. Make sure your molding is strong enough to hold the artwork and other contents it will contain.

If in doubt, keep the design simple. You can always change it later. Go by your own tastes and beliefs if you are framing for yourself. If you are doing it for someone else, try to reflect their tastes.

CUTTING A MITERED CORNER

1. Measure along the rabbet. Keep the rabbet toward you while you are measuring (Fig. 2-3) and while it is in the miter box. If you are using builder's molding, keep toward you the side on which you will add the parting strip.

2. Line up your measuring mark exactly with the guide lines that are part of your miter box (Fig. 2-4).

Fig. 2-3. *Keep the rabbet side of your frame toward you while measuring. With a sharp pencil, mark your cutting point.*

Fig. 2-4. *Pencil mark that is lined up exactly with the miter box guide line. Score the 45-degree angle marks on the scrap wood in the base of the miter box to help you line up the pencil marks on your molding.*

3. Hold the molding firmly. Visualize how it will look in the finished frame. You are cutting a diagonal line from an outside corner, pointing into the artwork in the finished frame.

Measure before you cut each time. Check against your measurements to make certain you are getting the right lengths. If both long lengths are exactly the same and both short lengths are exactly the same, you should have a frame that will have perfectly square corners.

NAILING CORNERS

In joining a frame, place the nails at one end of each stick of molding. The heavier the frame, the more nails you need, generally two to three per corner (Fig. 2-5).

CUTTING YOUR FIRST
FRAME USING BUILDER'S MOLDING

Except for adding a parting strip to the builder's molding, you will use the following steps when you cut your first frame using framer's molding. At this point, assume that you have measured, remeasured, and picked out wood that has no flaws, and that you have compensated for gouges and marks by buying extra wood so you can cut around the flaws.

☞ To help you visualize a mitered corner, take a picture off the wall and set it in front of you. By looking at a finished frame, you will see how the angles point into the artwork.

1. Set your saw in the 45-degree angle in your miter box.
2. Cut off the first of five pieces of waste wood from either end of your stick of molding. This is the first mitered cut for your first long side (Fig. 2-6). Remember, visualize your lengths of wood in relationship to a finished frame. All mitered cuts point inward, toward the artwork.
3. Measure and mark your first long side, on the inside, where the rabbet edge will be (Fig. 2-3). Your measurements are based on inside frame measurements, not on the overall outside frame measurement. Line up this mark in your miter box (see Fig. 2-4), making certain your saw is cutting the 45-degree angle that points into the artwork.
4. Switch positions of your saw in the miter box to cut off a second piece of waste wood (Fig. 2-7).
5. Take your first long side and hold it against the molding to be cut (Fig. 2-8). Line up the angled cuts so they are flush. Using the first long side as your guide, mark your uncut wood for the second long side. Make sure this mark is exactly in your saw sight on the miter box, then cut to get your second long piece.

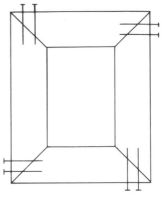

Nailing pattern

Fig. 2-5. *A diagram showing proper nailing of corners.*

Fig. 2-6. *The first piece of waste wood. This is necessary to get the correct angle, which points into the artwork.*

Fig. 2-7. *The second piece of waste wood. Remember to switch your saw for waste cuts.*

Fig. 2-8. *Measure your second piece of long wood by holding it against the first long side.*

6. Saw off the third piece of waste wood from your stick of molding by swinging the saw around again to the other mitered guide for 45-degree cuts.

7. Measure your first short side. Mark it on the inside as you did with the long side. Cut.

8. Swing the saw and remove the fourth triangle of waste wood.

9. Hold your first short side against the remaining stick of molding. Repeat step 5, marking your second short piece exactly the same as your first short piece. Cut.

ASSEMBLING YOUR WOOD FRAME

1. Figure 2-9 shows your four pieces, measured and cut, along with the waste wood.

2. Put one long side and one short side (Fig. 2-10) in a corner clamp or a miter vise. If they do not fit perfectly to form a corner without gaps, try switching pieces of wood. By experimenting with these four sides, you should achieve perfectly mitered corners. Add glue and brads.

☞ If you are trying to join two sides and discover you have a slight gap—not a lot, but a little (Fig. 2-11)—keep the two lengths in the vise and cut through the joint using a hacksaw (Fig. 2-12) with a very thin blade. This method will work if you are off less than ⅛ inch.

3. Loosen the short piece from the clamp. Apply glue with your finger or a piece of waste mat board to both areas that are to be glued together. Apply glue evenly. When pressed together in the vise or clamp, a hairline of glue should appear on the surface of the joint (Fig. 2-13). Wipe it off completely with a barely dampened sponge or paper towel.

4. Predrill nail holes (Fig. 2-14). Make sure you are using a bit that is smaller in diameter than the brad or nail you plan to use.

5. Add brads (Fig. 2-15). In this case, two are adequate. Stagger them slightly. Use common sense and the shape of the molding, to determine where to place the brads as well as how many to use.

6. Use your nail set (see Fig. 1-11). Tap each nail twice: once to set the vibrations into action and once to drive the nail home. Leave this corner in the corner clamp or transfer it to a miter vise, if you are using one.

7. Repeat steps 2 through 6 for the other two sides.

8. Join the two corners you have made to form the rectangular frame. Set a block of wood under the far side (Fig. 2-16) to keep your frame level while your hands are gluing and nailing the third corner.

9. Nail and set the final corner, keeping the opposite corner (that you have just joined) level by placing the block under it.

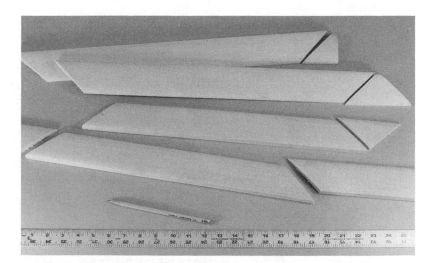

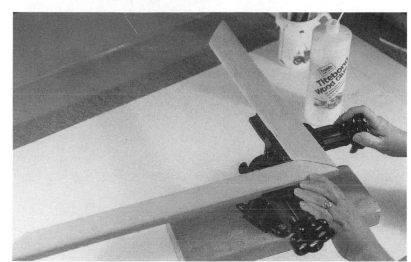

Fig. 2-9. *The four sides, with waste pieces, showing how a frame is cut from a single piece of molding.*

Fig. 2-10. *Align one long side (parallel to your body) and one short side (perpendicular to you) in the miter box for the mitering procedure.*

Fig. 2-11. *A mitered corner that doesn't quite make it.*

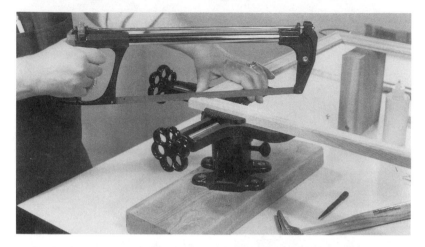

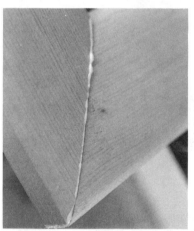

Fig. 2-12. *Sometimes a corner that is a little off can be corrected by sawing through the corner with a thin hacksaw blade, while holding the two pieces of wood firmly in a miter vise.*

Fig. 2-13. *(left) Glue should ooze out from the mitered corner and must be wiped clean quickly.*

Fig. 2-14. *(right) Predrill nail holes.*

Fig. 2-15. *Hammer in brads (also called nails).*

10. Use corner clamps or other forms of corner clamping (review Figs. 1-6, 1-8, 1-9, and 1-10) until the glue is set.

11. You might want to sand your frame, as well as fill the holes made by the nail set or pressure clamping. These steps will be discussed in Chapter 4, as well as in special projects.

MAKING A PARTING STRIP

When you are buying wood, remember that lumber is sized before it is milled, so the finished, or actual, size of a piece is smaller than the dimensions used for it. If you decide you need a ¾-inch parting strip, ask for a 1-inch strip, and so on.

1. On the underside of your builder's molding frame, mark a line ¼ to ½ inch in from the window opening (Fig. 2-17) and rule this all around. This will be the area of your rabbet. Install the parting strip using this line as your guide, and form a rabbet for the frame.

2. Figure 2-18 shows how to measure and cut your parting strips. Square off the end of your parting strip, using the 90-degree guide (or center) of your miter box. The basic formula to establish each of the four lengths of the parting strip follows: Take the width of the parting strip: ¾ inch. Add the width of the rabbet for both sides of the frame: ¼ inch × 2 = ½ inch. Add the length of the window openings. For a 11- × -14-inch opening, you will have two 14-inch lengths and two 11-inch lengths:

¾ inch + ½ inch + 14 inches = 15¼ inches. (You need two lengths, 15¼ inches each.) and ¾ inch + ½ inch + 11 inches = 12¼ inches. (You need two lengths, 12¼ inches each.)

3. Cut two 15¼-inch lengths and two 12¼-inch lengths from the ¾-inch parting strip wood.

4. Glue and nail these lengths directly to the back of the frame (Fig. 2-19). An alternative is to assemble the parting strip as a separate unit, and then glue and nail it to the back of the frame. (The first way described is easier.) If the parting strip will show and needs to be mounted flush with the frame, glue and nail the parting strip to the builder's molding (Fig. 2-20) before you make any saw cuts. Drive the nails only part of the way in, so you can remove them easily after the parting strip and molding have become bonded together. Then, measure it, miter it, and proceed as you would to make a frame using framer's molding.

CREATING A FRAME WITH FRAMER'S MOLDING

Cutting and assembling a frame with framer's molding is very similar to using builder's molding, and is generally easier because of the built-in rabbet.

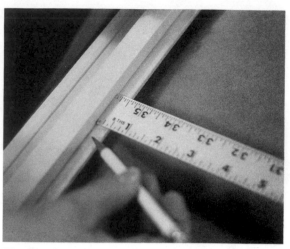

Fig. 2-16. *A block of scrap wood on the far side of your frame holds it level while you complete the frame.*

Fig. 2-17. *Measure and mark ¼ inch from the edge of the builder's molding for proper placement of parting strip.*

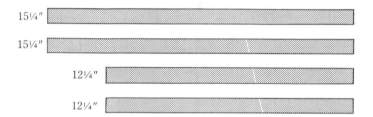

15¼″

15¼″

12¼″

12¼″

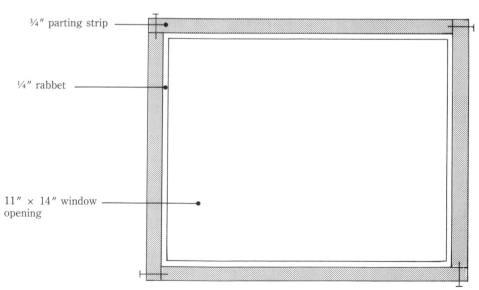

¾″ parting strip

¼″ rabbet

11″ × 14″ window opening

Fig. 2-18. *Diagram showing how to measure and place a parting strip.*

Fig. 2-19. *Glue the parting strip, then nail it to the back of the frame.*

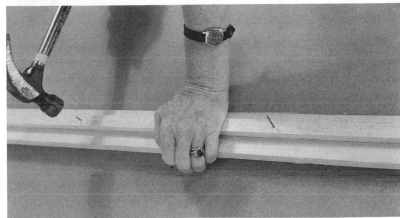

Fig. 2-20. *An optional way to add a parting strip is to glue it to the builder's molding, nail it and leave nails in until glue is set, and then saw the molding and parting strip in one operation. Remember to remove the nails before you start cutting, or you will damage your saw.*

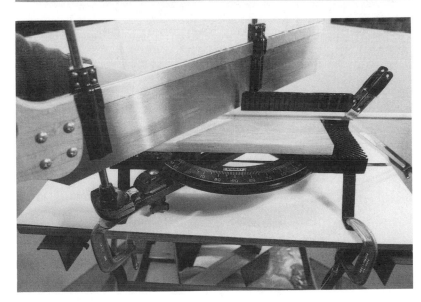

Fig. 2-21. *Cutting framer's molding. Note the clamp with protective plastic jaws holding the wood in position in the miter box.*

1. Measure your framing wood requirement the same as for builder's molding frame. For a 17-×-21-inch frame opening: Add the four sides: 17 inches + 17 inches + 21 inches + 21 inches = 76 inches. Add the allowance for waste wood cuts (assume molding is 1 inch wide): 8 × 1 inch = 8 inches. Add 1 inch for sawdust. The total is 85 inches: Divide that number by 12 inches to get the number of feet of molding you need. 85 ÷ 12 = 7 feet 1 inch. Therefore, you need 8 feet of framer's molding.

Fig. 2-22. *Framer's molding with waste wood.*

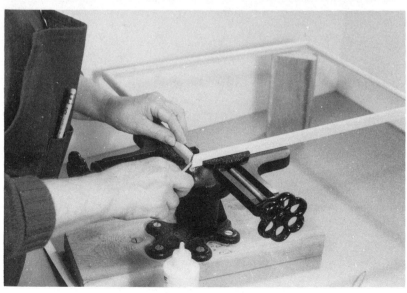

Fig. 2-23. *Assembling the final corners of the frame. A wood block on the opposite side holds the operation level with the miter vise.*

2. Cut the four sides (Figs. 2-21 and 2-22).

3. Join a long and a short side in the miter vise.

4. Glue and nail and use your nail set.

5. Join the other short side and long side and form your frame. Use a block of wood to hold your entire frame level while you are assembling the two corners to form your frame (Fig. 2-23). Remember to glue the opposite corners of the frame as well as the two you are working on. With well-fitted corners, you might not be able to apply the glue to the fourth corner after you have nailed the third corner.

3:
CUTTING MATS
AND
BACKBOARDS

The standard mat consists of two pieces of mat board of the same size, hinged with a strip of gummed linen tape along the top (Figs. 3-1 and 3-2). The backboard supports the artwork, and the mat in front has a window cut in it to display the artwork. The size of the window will vary with individual tastes.

The window mat should be thick enough to prevent the artwork and glazing from touching. If they do touch, condensation might occur, causing staining, mold growth, or other damage. Condensation causes watercolors to run, and photographs, prints, and other types of art to stick to the glass.

In most cases, the window mat overlaps the paper the artwork is on. The area of the art that is viewed through the mat opening is called the *sight measurement* (Fig. 3-3). The actual artwork, in many cases, is slightly larger than the sight measurement because of the slight overlap of the mat. If it is absolutely necessary for the entire work to be displayed, the window mat can be cut larger than the artwork. Then the artwork *floats,* and all edges are seen in the sight measurement. Floating might be necessary if the artwork is irregular in shape or if the artist insists that everything show to the very edge of the paper.

Mat boards come in regular, acid-free, or "rag." These types, in turn, are available in a variety of finishes and colors, as well as a wide assortment of textures and fabric coverings. Regular mat board is the one most commonly used, although conservation matting is increasingly being used. (This subject will be covered in more detail in the projects section.) The key difference is the cost. In addition, the less expensive regular mat board contains acids that find their way through migration from the bevel cut onto the artwork. These acids can stain the art permanently. Because most framing is not meant to last forever, this is not as horrible as it seems. You should not be

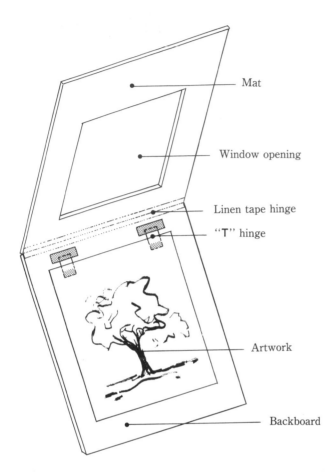

Mat

Window opening

Linen tape hinge

"T" hinge

Artwork

Backboard

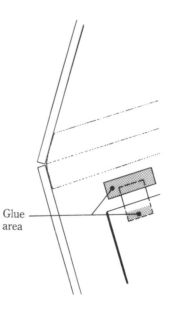

Glue area

Fig. 3-1. *Hinging a window mat to a backing board with linen tape.*

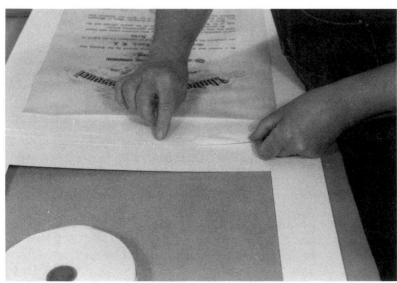

Fig. 3-2. *Taping a window mat to backing board with linen tape.*

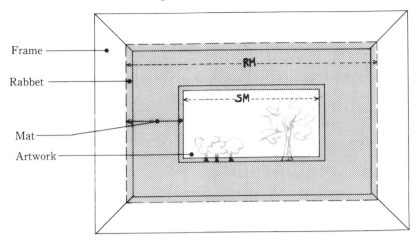

RM = rabbet measurement
SM = sight measurement

Frame

Rabbet

Mat

Artwork

¼" of mat is hidden by rabbet
¼" of art is hidden by mat

Fig. 3-3. *Sight measurement is that area of a photograph or artwork that is visible to the viewer. In most cases, approximately ¼ inch of art disappears under the mat board all around. Note that the mat board extends from under the rabbet to over the art.*

too concerned when you are matting an inexpensive print with regular mat board.

Mats covered with fabric are discussed in Chapter 10. They are easy to work with and offer an inexpensive way to add a fascinating new look to your work.

HOW TO MEASURE MATS FOR CUTTING

Accuracy in measuring is important throughout the framing process. Because your mat offers you the greatest opportunity to enhance your artwork, the importance of measuring cannot be stressed too much.

Once you have established the frame size, your next decision is how large to make the opening for the mat. If you are not floating the art, and because paper will expand or contract in time, leave enough overlap to prevent the artwork from popping out of the mat opening. The overlap should be ¼ inch on most artwork and ⅜ inch on larger works.

☞ Wash your hands before you handle mats. Most people do not realize how easily the normal oil from their hands can transfer onto mats and ruin them.

CUTTING A MAT

Tools you will need: a metal ruler that can double as a straightedge, a sharp pencil, an eraser, a razor, a utility knife, and a mat cutter.

A mat cutter is an essential tool. An optional tool is a marking gauge (Fig. 3-4).

1. Look at your artwork and decide what size mat would look best: one inch? two inches? three inches? Do you want the same measurement on all sides, or would you like the bottom to be slightly larger? The example shows a mat that is equal on all sides. The mat overlaps the edges of the artwork by ¼ inch, and approximately ¼ inch of the mat will disappear all around the frame under the rabbet.

For example, artwork that measures 10 × 13 inches will have a sight measurement of 9½ × 12½ inches, since you need a ¼-inch overlap to hold it under the edges of your mat window. If you use a 2-inch mat, ¼ inch of that mat will disappear behind the rabbet measurement all around. To compensate, measure in 2¼ inches on all sides of a 14- × -17-inch mat board, then mark a cutting line that will be your window. This compensation provides a 2-inch mat around all four sides of the artwork, with ¼ inch disappearing under the rabbet.

2. With a paper cutter or a utility knife, cut your backboard from a large sheet of mat board.

3. On the second piece of 14- × -17-inch mat board, which is going to be your window mat, mark your cutting lines on the reverse using a marking gauge (as shown in Fig. 3-5) or a pencil and ruler.

4. Put a slash mark (Fig. 3-6) across one of the lines you are going to cut. This example will have a double mat equidistant all around. The slash mark will help you to reposition the center, or *dropout*, later.

5. Clamp your ruler to your work area, along with your mat board and an extra strip of scrap board (Fig. 3-7). The scrap board acts as a slip sheet under the cutting edge where the blade will be cutting through the mat board. This extra piece keeps the blade sharp and compresses the two boards together to provide a clean bevel. Insert the blade on the cutting line. Stand firm and make a decisive, deep, one-sweep cut, pulling the mat cutter directly toward you (Fig. 3-8). When you loosen the clamp to swing your mat around for the other three cuts, be sure to move the slip sheet each time. You do not want the blade to slip into the same groove twice, or you might get a ragged edge.

6. Following the same procedure, cut the other three sides. The center will drop out, leaving your window opening. If your cuts are not quite complete, finish cutting the bevel carefully with a razor blade. Work from the front of the mat (Fig. 3-9).

7. After checking to see that the bevel is accurately cut, place the dropout back in place, aligning with the slash mark. Use an adhesive-tape gun (ATG gun) to attach pressure-sensitive tape all around the window (Fig. 3-10). Place a small amount in the center to keep the dropout in place while you cut your second mat.

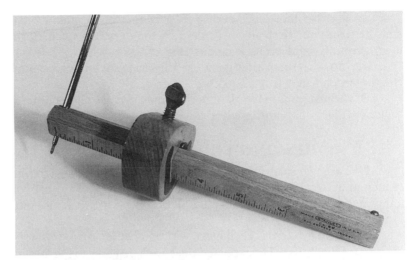

Fig. 3-4. *A marking gauge is another optional tool that can make your job easier. It can be sold as a carpenter's tool, but the scribe can be replaced with an erasable ballpoint pen filler or a pencil. This one has settings from less than 1 to 6 inches. It marks the cutting line perfectly, with one swift gesture per line, and is very good for mats that are to be cut from the back of the mat board.*

Fig. 3-5. *(right) Marking gauge; marking on reverse side of mat board.*

Fig. 3-6. *(bottom left) A slash mark, crossing the cut line between the window mat and dropout piece, makes it possible to replace your dropout into the exact area where it came from—a necessary step in cutting double mats. (This mark has been made darker so it would be seen for this project.)*

Fig. 3-7. *(bottom right) Clamping the slip sheet, mat, and straightedge prior to using the mat cutter.*

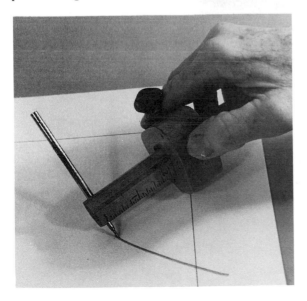

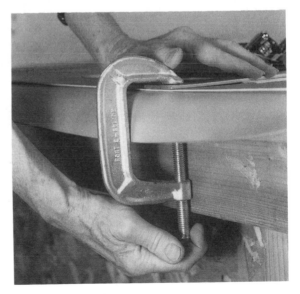

8. For the liner, cut another piece of mat board about 1 inch smaller than your first piece. Place it on top of your first mat, line it up carefully, and press it against the adhesive.

9. Move the marking gauge setting in ½ inch and mark and cut the second mat (Fig. 3-11).

10. Adjust your artwork under the mat, sighting it through the window (Fig. 3-12), and apply the T hinges.

HINGING YOUR ARTWORK

1. Take two small lengths of linen tape (about 1 inch long), moisten ⅛ inch of one end of each, and stick them to the back of the artwork a few inches from each edge (Fig. 3-13). For larger artwork, use more hinges.

2. Make a T across each hinge with another length of moistened linen tape (Fig. 3-14). The first hinge will be adhered only to the artwork. The cross-piece will hold that hinge and, consequently, the artwork to the backing board. This type of hinging permits the artwork to breathe, or expand and contract, without buckling within the frame when it reacts to changes in humidity.

3. Close the window frame over the artwork. You now have a matted piece of artwork, ready for insertion behind the glass of the frame.

Fig. 3-8. *Pull the Logan cutter toward the body while cutting the mat.*

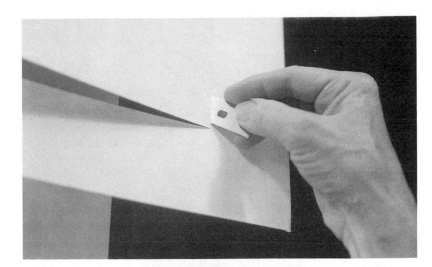

Fig. 3-9. *A razor blade can finish the cut if a corner is not quite complete. Work from the face of the mat.*

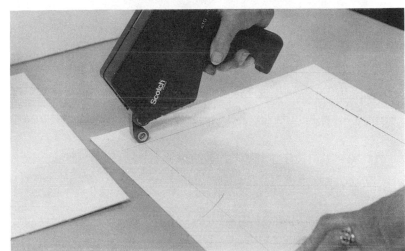

Fig. 3-10. *An ATG gun dispenses adhesive around the window area of the mat.*

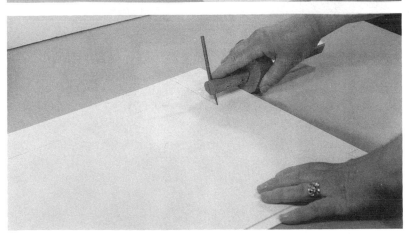

Fig. 3-11. *A marking gauge marks the lines to cut for the liner mat.*

Fig. 3-12. *Position the art under a mat.*

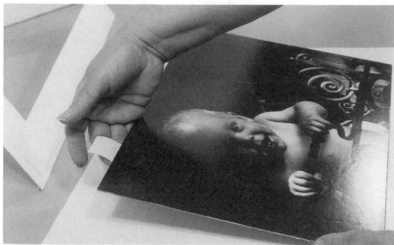

Fig. 3-13. *Apply a hinge to back of art.*

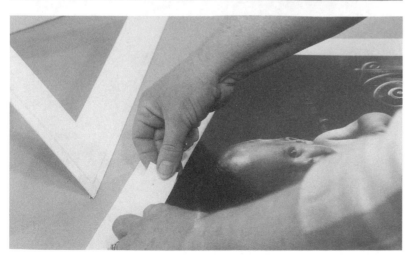

Fig. 3-14. *Apply a cross hinge to form a* T *with the first vertical hinge.*

4:
COMPLETING THE FRAMING

Some people are afraid of cutting glass, probably because they have never cut any. With a little practice, this process can become quite easy.

GLASS CUTTING

Economics enters into glass cutting, like everything else. The really foolproof glass cutters are wall mounted and professional framers use them. A lot of professionals still use the hand-held type, however, either one with a diamond point or the less expensive cutter with a rotary steel cutting edge that must be stored in oil or kerosene. A newer, self-lubricating cutter is also available. (Three basic cutters are shown in Fig. 1-16.) Neither the diamond cutter nor the self-lubricating one needs special storage arrangements.

To cut glass:

1. Mark your glass with a felt-tipped pen or marker (Fig. 4-1).
2. Place the glass on a flat, lint-free, smooth surface. Pull the glass cutter toward you, using a steel straightedge as a guide (Fig. 4-2).
3. Do not score the glass a second time. Make one firm, clean stroke and run the line off the edge of the glass. You don't need to use as much pressure as you might think.
4. Break the glass in a clean, deliberate snap, using the corner of a table (Fig. 4-3) as your guide.

☞ Glass has a memory. It must be snapped free of the scored line within two minutes or less, or it will cure itself.

Except for oils and some fabrics, you will want to cover and protect your artwork with glass or Plexiglas. Picture-framing glass is thinner than regular glass, and more expensive, but your hardware store might not stock it. Regular, single-strength glass is fine, and less expensive.

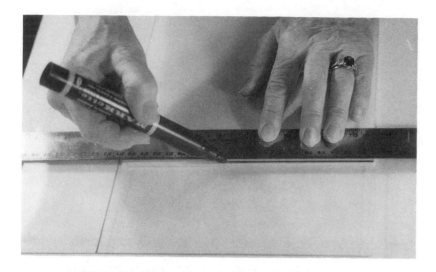

Fig. 4-1. *Use a marker to indicate where to score glass.*

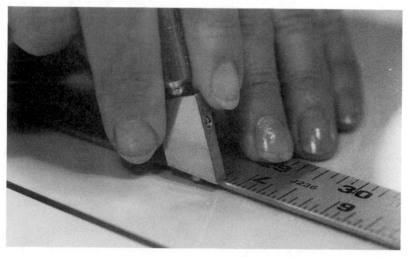

Fig. 4-2. *Scoring glass.*

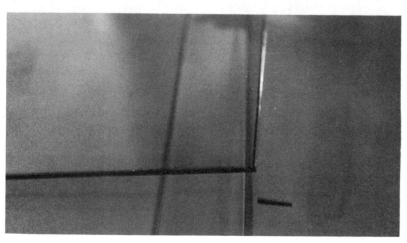

Fig. 4-3. *Snapping glass free.*

40

You can frame most artwork using single-strength glass. If the artwork is to be hung in a living room or office with wall-to-wall windows, you might want to consider using nonglare glass, which is much more expensive. Under such conditions, nonglare glass might be worth using if you want your artwork to be seen. Some say nonglare glass "fuzzes" the artwork. On some reproductions, it might in fact enhance it, making the artwork look better than it really is. There is also a new crystal clear antireflective glass on the market called Denglas that is often used in museums over oils. You do not know the glass is even there. Just as nonglare is considerably more expensive than regular or picture glass, Denglas is considerably more expensive than nonglare. For that special place or certain types of art, however, you might want to pay the price.

Don't store glass casually. It scratches easily, and once it has a scratch or mark on it, you won't want to use it in framing. Also, check glass carefully when you buy it to make certain it has no flaws before you cut it.

☞ Some framers use a brush dipped in kerosene to coat their cutting line before running the glass cutter down it, whether using the rotary steel or diamond-tipped cutter. This gives a cleaner break.

PLEXIGLAS

Acrylic glazing or Plexiglas, which is much lighter than glass and is available in both regular and nonglare, comes in various weights and thicknesses. The thicker it is, the more expensive, which does not mean it is better. Plexiglas should never be used on charcoals, pastels, or graphite drawings. The static electricity inherent in the material acts as a magnet, and you might end up with an image on your glazing.

The two big disadvantages are that Plexiglas attracts dust and scratches very easily. Still, it is very useful when dealing with large works of art that need glazing, where glass would make the art too heavy, or when transporting a work of art from place to place or show to show. It is usually less expensive to buy one piece of Plexiglas than two pieces of glass. It is also excellent, and sometimes essential, when shipping a work of art. The San Francisco Museum of Modern Art ships most of its loan works in metal frames using acrylic glazing.

To cut Plexiglas, peel back the protective plastic sheeting to where you want to make your cut. Place the Plexiglas on a flat, lint-free surface. Take a steel ruler or straightedge and clamp it to a table with the Plexiglas under the ruler. With a special Plexiglas cutter, score the Plexiglas several times, then snap it off. The deeper the score, the easier it is to make the break.

Plexiglas also comes with a protective sheet of paper stuck to it. You can cut the Plexiglas with this paper still on it. When you buy this type, use it right away because the paper becomes a permanent part of the Plexiglas if left on for any length of time.

To clean Plexiglas, use a soft cloth and special Plexiglas cleaner that can be purchased in supermarkets or hardware stores. Never use ammonia-based glass cleaner or paper towels.

Place the Plexiglas on a clean surface, such as a new piece of mat board, when working with it. Otherwise, its magnetic attraction will lure every piece of dust in the area. Once you try to "fit" the frame, you'll have your hands full trying to get rid of all those little bits of lint and dust from the surface of the Plexiglas or the mat.

FINISHING YOUR FRAMES

Because entire books have been published on how to finish wood, only a few relatively simple but effective finishes will be covered here. Finishes are also a matter of taste and will vary as much as the type of artwork you like. When applicable, finishes are discussed in specific projects.

The Natural Look

Always prepare your wood by sanding the surface smooth, eliminating scratches, rough spots, and surface imperfections. Use a basic sealant—an inexpensive one is shellac with a little alcohol—or a commercial product that will not stain or darken the wood. After sealing the wood, rub down the surface again with steel wool or very fine sandpaper.

The simplest way to get a natural look is to use wax. Wrap a soft cloth around a small ball of paste wax. The heat of your hand will help you apply it to the frame. Be generous. Buff it. Repeat the process until you are happy with the results. Many frames look terrific with just a wax shine that brings out the deep, rich look of the grain. If there is little or no grain, you still get a beautiful finish that flatters most artwork.

☞ Save all scraps of wood when you are building a frame. You can test different finishes on these scraps. You might change your mind about some finishes once you've seen how they look on different types of woods. Then you'll be glad you tried it on scrap wood first rather than on your frame.

A Natural But Darker Look

There are many easy-to-use products that you brush on with a cloth, let set, and then wipe off. With repeated applications you can get darker tones. With some finishes, the longer you let it set, the darker it gets. Once you've experimented with scrap wood and done a frame or two, you will know how to achieve the desired effects.

Metallic Finishes

There are several easy ways to get a beautiful metallic finish. One is to use an aerosol spray. Another is to apply a finish with your fingers or a soft cloth, rub it into the wood, and buff it off. The commercial names for the latter are often a description of how you use them, such as Rub 'n Buff. Both the spray and rubbing give you excellent finishes. Try both to see which you prefer.

Painting

With the convenience of aerosol containers, you can paint your frames almost any color you want, either glossy or matte finishes. There are more economical ways, but what spraying saves in time and the elimination of brush strokes and clean-up more than makes up for the cost when you are painting just a few frames. There is the problem of finding a place where you can confine the spray, however. If an outdoor area is available, it is ideal (Figs. 4-4 and 4-5).

One answer to how to confine the aerosol spray is to use a large cardboard container or build a paint shelter out of cardboard (Fig. 4-6). Cover the back with kraft or newspaper while you are spraying, so you can reuse the container. If you are spraying a frame, place two nails near the top to hang your frame on while spraying. This shelter can be used inside in bad weather, if you are careful. The sides will keep the spray from drifting, but you still must be careful not to inhale the fumes. Be sure there is adequate ventilation and wear a painter's mask. Follow the directions on the can.

☞ Place a pushpin in the four corners of the underside of your frame (Fig. 4-7). This will keep the edges of the frame from sticking to the surface where it is drying.

Some people still prefer to paint with a brush. It is not all that inconvenient and is definitely the least expensive way of getting a painted surface. Water-based paints are vastly improved, and even cleaning up with solvents is not that much of a problem. Again, use scrap wood to sample your paint before you paint a completed frame (Fig. 4-8). Stay away from high-gloss enamel, unless you have the talent to use this beautiful paint without leaving brush strokes. It is very frustrating to use if you don't have the knack.

☞ Throwaway plastic gloves are an excellent investment to use when finishing (see Fig. 4-8).

Brushes

Another area where many people make wrong decisions is in underestimating the importance of proper brushes. You need one with

Fig. 4-4. *Spraying a completed frame.*

Fig. 4-5. *(left) Use kraft paper to protect area when spraying a frame. It is difficult to get sides and inner areas while holding the frame. Propping up the frame (with rocks or something under the paper) helps.*

Fig. 4-6. *(bottom left) Improvised paint shelter for spraying.*

Fig. 4-7. *(bottom right) A pushpin keeps paint from sticking to the paper surface while paint dries.*

natural bristles for oil-based paints, stains, or varnishes for a truly beautiful job. The synthetic brushes are fine for latex water-based paints.

Be sure to use the correct solvents to clean your brushes after working, and clean them right away or don't bother. Check the directions that come with the particular brand of paint or finish you are using. In general, use turpentine to clean brushes after painting with oil or varnish, denatured alcohol after using shellac, and lacquer thinner after using lacquer.

Other Finishes

There are other simple and quick-dry methods of finishing. *Gesso* is a versatile product and is especially good with soft woods. Use several diluted coatings and sand the finish between applications (Fig. 4-9). Urethane, vinyls, and other new types of finishes are easy to apply, but be sure to test finishes you are not entirely familiar with and follow directions. Many finishes are further enhanced with an application of clear wax after they have been completely rubbed down and pumiced. Experiment with various finishes (Fig. 4-10). You will probably find one or two that will appeal to you, which you'll use on most of your frames. If you have not used foam pad applicators, try them. They do not leave brush marks, and you might be successful using these where you have not been able to get a satisfactory job with a brush. Try it on test wood first, however, before you attack a frame that you have special plans for. Never get upset because you can't get a specific type of finish to look right. There's always another one you can use to get beautiful results.

FITTING YOUR FRAME

You've made your frame, cut your mats, and positioned the artwork. The glass is cut, and now you are ready to put it all together.

1. Clean the glass.

2. Make sure your frame is free of dust. A blast from an aerosol can of air is suggested, especially to reach the far corners of the rabbet. Place the frame face down. Put the glass on the rabbet in the frame.

☞ Place a rug or similar lint-free material under the frame while fitting. It will cut down on glass breakage.

3. Place mat and artwork on top of glass facing the front of the frame.

4. Filler board comes next. You can use various thicknesses of foam core or large pieces of mat board. This should hold the artwork firmly, but not too tightly; remember, both glass and paper need room to breathe.

Fig. 4-8. *Test paint for finish. Note the wise use of disposable plastic gloves.*

Fig. 4-9. *Gesso with paint brush and paints for tinting gesso plus makeshift texturizing tools (including broken comb, which worked well.)*

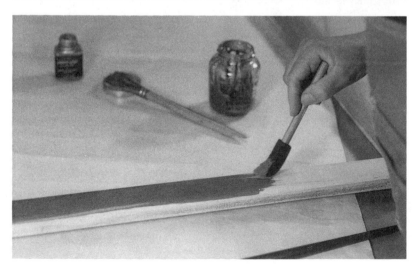

Fig. 4-10. *Try different strengths of finishes using foam pad applicators.*

Fig. 4-11. *Pliers are used to force nails into the back of the frame to hold the contents.*

Fig. 4-12. *(above, left) Apply adhesive to back of frame.*

Fig. 4-13. *(above, right) Place kraft paper into position as dust cover of frame.*

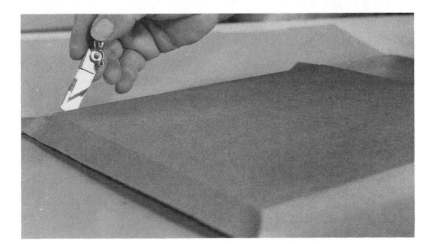

Fig. 4-14. *Trim excess paper using a professional trimming tool.*

Fig. 4-15. *Fasten screw eyes about one-third down the sides of the frame and insert the wire into the loop of the screw eye.*

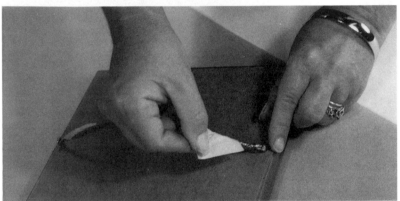

Fig. 4-16. *Masking tape protects fingers from ends of hanging wires.*

Fig. 4-17. *Corner bumpers hold picture away from wall, allowing air to circulate.*

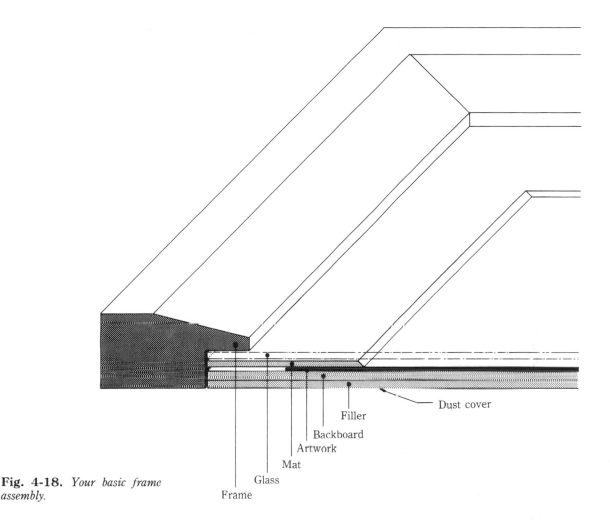

Fig. 4-18. *Your basic frame assembly.*

Dust cover

Filler

Backboard

Artwork

Mat

Glass

Frame

5. Place brads or nails in position and force them into the frame with pliers (Fig. 4-11). In the special projects that follow, other tools will be demonstrated.

6. Cover the edges of the frame with glue (Fig. 4-12).

7. Tear or cut a sheet of kraft paper to approximate size, spray or sprinkle it lightly with water, and place it in position over the glued area (Fig. 4-13).

8. Trim off the excess paper (Fig. 4-14).

9. Place screw eyes approximately one-third of the distance down on the back. Use an awl to push a slight indentation so the screw eye will enter easily. On harder woods, predrill this hole.

10. Fasten the screw eyes. Insert the wire (Fig. 4-15), twist it, and insert it into the screw eye on the opposite side. Thread the wire twice through the loop of the screw eye before twisting.

11. Cover the end wires with masking tape (Fig. 4-16) to protect fingers while handling the picture.

12. Place bumpers on the bottom corners (Fig. 4-17) to allow air to circulate in back of the frame.

13. When you are purchasing hanging wire or hooks, read the manufacturer's statement carefully as to the suggested weights recommended that the product will hold.

14. Figure 4-18 shows a basic frame assembly.

5:
MAKING TWO BASIC FRAMES

These tools and materials are very basic to most framing projects. In the chapters that follow, you will be referred back to these as well as to some optional tools.

Materials

artwork • brads • filler board • glass • glue (Sobo's and Elmer's white and regular wood glue) • kraft paper • mat board • masking tape (for ends of hanging wire) • screw eyes • wire • wood (builder's molding, framer's molding, parting strip) • wood finishes (Rub 'n Buff Gold Leaf and Treasure Gold pewter)

Tools

aerosol can of air • ATG dispenser (adhesive transfer gun) • awl • break-starting pliers • corner clamps • cinch clamps • pressure C clamps • spring clamps • Dexter mat cutter • electric drill • felt-tipped pen • glass cutter • Logan mat cutter • marking gauge • miter box and saw • miter vise • nail set • pencil • pliers • Pro-Trim knife (paper trimmer for edge of dust covers) • razor blade • rulers • straightedge • metal square • tack hammer

The following projects include step-by-step procedures on how to frame two prints, starting from scratch and ending with two completed frames you could hang in your living room. The first is done with a double mat and builder's molding that needs the addition of a parting strip. The second uses framer's molding and a single mat.

After you have read through these projects, you will be well on your way to tackling any framing job. The projects that follow refer to the tools and materials used here as well as instructions on basic framing and matting in Chapters 1 and 2. New tools and materials will be listed for new projects at the beginning of each chapter and explained in more detail, if necessary, when they are used. Optional tools are also mentioned, not to endorse their use, but to let you know they exist. (And there are many more not used here; check supplier's catalogs.)

Chapter 1 listed basic tools and some optional ones. "Optional" means just that: you can still use regular glue instead of a spray or an ATG gun (adhesive dispenser), and a razor blade can still do the same job as a professional trimming knife to cut away excess kraft paper on dust covers.

Whenever you have a piece of artwork you intend to frame, think out the entire project before you even pick up a saw or mat cutter. Consider the artwork first. If it is a work of art on paper, it probably will need glazing. Ask yourself, then, will I use one or two mats or some kind of spacer to keep the artwork from touching the glazing? Normally you will answer these questions yourself. In these learning projects, however, basic decisions are made for you, showing as many different situations as possible to help you develop your framing skills.

All other projects in this book are more or less variations on the two in this chapter. They are planned to help you expand your talent and imagination and to apply your skills to each new project you encounter.

FRAMING THE HOPPER REPRODUCTION

The first project is to frame a Hopper reproduction (Fig. 5-1, left). Because this is a print on paper, it will be framed under glass. Your first decision is to choose a mat to protect and enhance this print. We selected a bright blue for the outside mat and a brilliant white

Fig. 5-1. *This Hopper reproduction will be framed under glass.*

the inside or liner mat. The blue reflects Hopper's use of vivid blue throughout the painting, and the white picks up the sails and the lighthouse.

Next, select a framing molding. Because this is a first project, choose a simple builder's molding that fits flat in the miter box. A ¾-inch parting strip provides ample room for glass, double mat, artwork, and filler board (Fig. 5-2).

For a finish, pick a gold that is easy to apply and reflects the colors in Hopper's painting. Assume that you have already cut the builder's molding and have scrap pieces to try out several finishes. After a few rejections, you select Rub 'n Buff Gold Leaf, a decorative wood finish. Trying it on the wood sample proved that it is not only easy to apply, but provides the complementary look without calling attention to itself.

Cutting the Frame

The basic decisions have now been made. The rabbet measurement is 11⅛ × 14⅛ inches. The builder's molding must be cut 10⅞ × 13⅞ inches.

1. Measure your builder's molding and parting strip requirements as discussed in Chapter 1, then cut off the first piece of waste wood on the builder's molding. This gives you your first mitered cut, pointing into the artwork.

☞ Remember the earlier tip to take a framed picture off the wall and keep it in front of you while you are reading instructions as well as when you are sawing your first frame. It will help you visualize what you are doing.

Fig. 5-2. *Parting strip and builder's molding that is similar to that used to frame the Hopper print.*

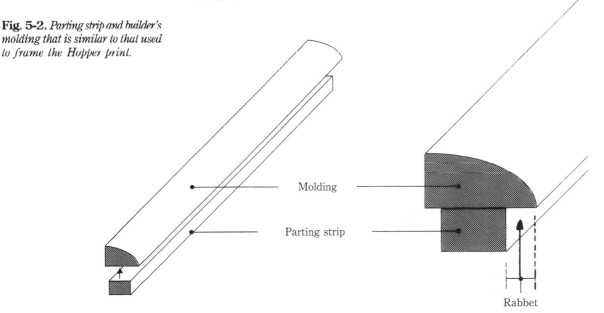

Molding

Parting strip

Rabbet

2. Measure from the inside of this piece of framing wood (not the part where the point is) and mark off where 13⅞ inches will fall. Move your saw in the miter box from the position where you took off the first piece of waste wood to the other 45-degree angle guide. Place the pencil mark, which shows where 13⅞ inches is on the wood, directly in the sight of this guideline on your miter box. Cut. This gives you your first long side.

3. Swing the saw over to the other 45-degree guide groove and cut your second piece of waste wood. This will be approximately twice as big a triangle as your first piece. (These instructions assume you do not have flaws in the molding. In reality, inspect your wood with every cut to make sure you do not end up with a frame with imperfections in the wood.)

4. Hold the first long side of framing wood up against the strip of molding (from which you cut the second piece of waste wood), directly up against the first long side, back to back.

5. Draw a line across the diagonal with a pencil on the uncut wood at the other end of your first long side. Bring the mark around onto the front of the rabbet, so that you can line up this mark in your miter box guide sight. Then line up the mark and cut your second long side.

6. Switch the saw again to the other 45-degree angle groove and cut the third piece of waste wood. (Until you are used to swinging your saw back and forth between these two guides, stop and think out each cut. Does the miter point in? This process is confusing for everyone at first.)

7. Measure and mark your first short side, cut it, and repeat the processes you have just used in cutting your two long sides. In this case, make them 10⅞ inches long. Figure 5-3 shows the fourth strip being cut, with the three waste pieces to the left of the strips that will form the frame. Notice the wood in Fig. 5-3 is shown in the sequence that it will be assembled and not in the sequence of cutting.

8. Using corner clamps, assemble the frame. Remember to apply glue to both pieces being mitered together for firmer bonding. After nailing, use a spring clamp (Fig. 5-4) to hold the corners while they are drying and the parting strips are being cut (Fig. 5-5). Because the parting strips form the rabbet behind the builder's molding and are not seen, it is not necessary to miter the corners. Instead, cut 90-degree angles and butt the wood together under the frame.

9. You have now assembled your basic frame, mitered the corners, and reinforced the glued miters with brads. Place the frame face down and mark the underside of the frame where the parting strips will be placed to form a rabbet. Measure in ¼ inch all the way around the inside of the frame. Glue each parting strip (Fig. 5-6) to the underside of the frame. For closer bonding, use pressure clamps and reinforce the glue with brads (Fig. 5-7).

Fig. 5-3. *Four pieces of builder's molding cut to 14-inch and 11-inch lengths.*

Fig. 5-4. *Apply clip-type spring clamp to the fourth corner of the frame in the miter vise.*

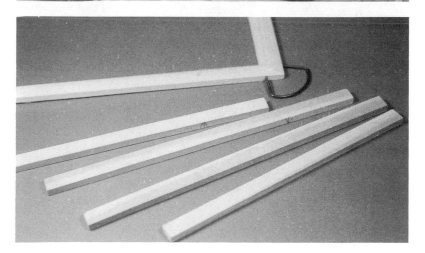

Fig. 5-5. *Four pieces of parting strip. Clamp is left in frame in the background until the glue is set.*

10. Finish the frame with the Rub 'n Buff Gold Leaf. Set the frame aside while you cut the mats and glass.

11. Measure and cut your backboard to 11 × 14 inches with a utility knife. Cutting this first will give you a triple check. If it fits, you know your frame is squared off properly and that these measurements are correct for cutting the window mats and glass. If it is slightly off, you can change the basic requirements slightly, and then cut your mats and glass.

Cutting the Double Mat

The 11-×-14-inch backing board gives the dimensions for the outside of the blue mat. By placing the Hopper print on the 11-×-14-inch backing board you can decide that the sight measurement, or area of the print that is visible through the window mat, will be 8⅜ × 11⅜ inches.

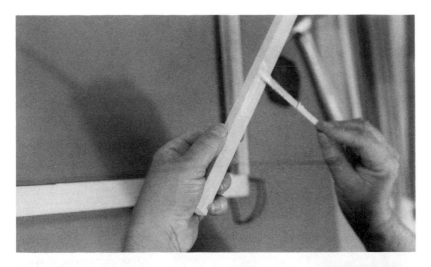

Fig. 5-6. *Apply glue with a scrap of mat board to the parting strip.*

Fig. 5-7. *Add brads to reinforce glued corners. In background, note the pressure spring clamps with vinyl grips that hold the wood in position without marring the wood surface.*

The final mat width will be 2½ inches all around. Before cutting the blue mat, glue the print to the center of the backing board with a white glue such as Elmer's or Sobo, both all-purpose glues.

As the sight measurement is relatively small, the inner mat will be only ³⁄₁₆ inches wide. Keep both measurements in mind before starting to cut the first mat.

1. Mark the area for the blue mat with a marking gauge (see Chap. 3, Fig. 3-4). This can be done with a ruler and a sharp pencil as well. To find the size of the first cut, mark off the 2½-inch overall mat size, then back off ³⁄₁₆ inches (the width of the inner mat), and make the first mark where you will cut with your mat cutter. (With the marking gauge, you move backward from 2½ to 2⁵⁄₁₆ inches.) Rule these four outside lines, making sure that they go from edge to edge on the back side of the mat. Put a slash mark on one side to act as a guide later. (The first dropout must be put back into exact position when you cut the liner or white mat.)

2. Make sure you have scrap board under the mat board, as you line up your straightedge and clamp it to the side of your workbench. This not only keeps you from cutting into your bench, but helps keep your blade sharp and accurate. Place your mat, marked for cutting, under the straightedge. Line up the straightedge with your drawn line and the top mark of the Logan mat cutter. (When measuring, follow the instructions of the specific cutter you are using. They vary with different models.)

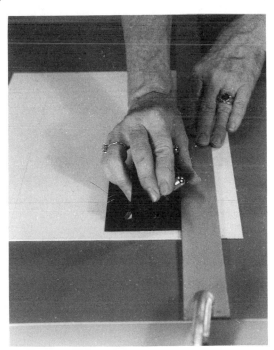

Fig. 5-8. *Starting to cut a mat using the guide on the side of the Logan cutter.*

Fig. 5-9. *The dropout falls away clean. Note the slash mark that will be used to reposition the dropout after the bevel is examined.*

Fig. 5-10. *Measure to establish where to cut the outer dimension of the liner mat.*

Fig. 5-11. *The finished double mat.*

3. Your work is on the right-hand side of the cutter. Push down firmly (Fig. 5-8) on the cutter and pull toward you until the lower line of the cutter is lined up with the lower line you have drawn on the mat. Move on and cut the three other sides. The dropout should fall out clean.

4. Pick up the mat, turn it over, and inspect it. If it is not cut through, use a single-edge razor blade or X-Acto knife (a razor-like cutting tool) to gently finish cutting the area still attached. Work from the front (see Fig. 3-9).

5. Put the dropout back into position (Fig. 5-9), lining it up with the slash mark. Put a dab of adhesive in the center of the dropout and all around the center of the mat with an ATG gun.

6. Measure to determine the outer dimensions of the liner (inner) mat (Fig. 5-10). Position the liner mat. It does not have to be the full 11 × 14 inches. If you have been cutting other mats, you might have smaller pieces of white mat available. Place the mat face down on the adhesive.

7. Take your marker or ruler and measure and mark the original overall size of the mat—2½ inches. Cut the 2½-inch mat following the same procedure as the first mat. Both centers now fall out. You have finished your double mat (Fig. 5-11).

Cutting the Glass and Fitting the Frame

1. Cut your glass to the same size as your backing board. Be certain your glass is clean.

☞ For a perfect, inexpensive glass cleaner: mix together 1 tablespoon rottenstone, 1 tablespoon mild dishwashing detergent, 1 cup methyl alcohol, and 2 quarts water. Shake well. Looks dreadful. Works wonders. Use with spray bottle with lint-free cloth.

2. Place the clean glass over the backing board so that two sides line up. Using a felt-tipped pen, mark the other two sides where you will cut the glass.

3. With a slow and steady pressure, cut a score line down the marked line using a glass cutter and a straightedge to guide you (Fig. 5-12). Score the glass just once. Sever the glass. In this case, a special pair of break-starting pliers with a humped lower jaw were used (Fig. 5-13). Remember that glass "cures" itself if not snapped within two minutes or less. These pliers facilitate snapping the glass free, especially on narrow strips, but they are not absolutely necessary. You can still snap glass over the edge of a table.

4. Your backing board has already been cut. A filler must go between the backing board and your dust cover. After recleaning the glass, blast a shot of air from an aerosol can to get excess dust or pieces of foreign matter out of the framing area. The job is now ready to be fitted or completed.

5. Use something resilient under the job while working at this stage, such as an old blanket or a piece of carpeting. On this soft but firm surface, place your filler board. Here a piece of mat board was thick enough. Foam core could have been used, if the space were deeper. Remember to never use ordinary corrugated board as it will eventually stain because of its acid content.

6. On top of the filler board, place your backing board with the artwork mounted to it, then the double mats, and then the glass. Place your frame on top of the whole package (Fig. 5-14). Grasp carefully and turn it all over.

7. Put four brads in the four centers of the frame, fitting them in with the head of the pliers. Check the front again to make sure that no dust or anything else has slipped in, such as an insect. (If something is there, pull out the four holding brads, remove the contents, and start over, blasting the glass with air from your aerosol can again.) If the frame is clean, put the rest of the brads in from the back side.

8. Cut a sheet of kraft paper slightly larger than the frame. After running the ATG gun around the back of the frame, put the kraft paper into position and press against the adhesive. Trim the excess paper off with a razor blade (Fig. 5-15), a utility knife, or a Pro-Trim knife (a professional trimmer).

9. Measure about a third of the way down on the parting strip and add screw eyes, using an awl (Fig. 5-16) or small drill to start the screws. With soft pine, you can probably start them by forcing them with your thumb and forefinger. Screw in the screw eyes, thread the wire, winding the end through each eye a second time. Finish off the ends of the hanging wire by winding them around the wire next to the hardware. Cover the ragged wire ends with masking tape.

☞ Once you have selected a screw eye, check it with a piece of scrap wood to make sure it doesn't come out through the outside profile of the wood or punch through into the inner part of the frame.

FRAMING WITH FRAMER'S MOLDING

For the second part of this learning project, a reprint of a photograph will be framed (see Fig. 5-1, right). Because it is a print on paper, again it will be framed under glass. The image, or sight measurement, of the print will be $6\frac{1}{2} \times 5$ inches.

☞ Although it can be easily done, artwork should not touch glass in a frame. Moisture will form, wrinkles or puckers are likely to appear, colors will run, and prints will stick.

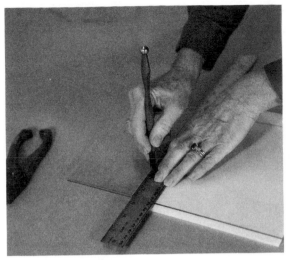

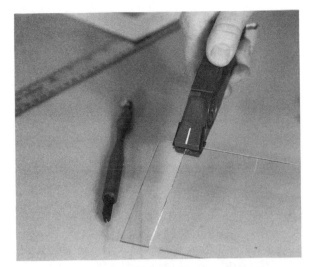

Fig. 5-12. *(above, left) Scoring glass.*

Fig. 5-13. *(above, right) Breaking off glass using a break starting pliers, an optional tool. Note new self-lubricating glass cutter in background.*

Fig. 5-14. *The frame, glass, artwork, backboard, and filler for the Hopper project.*

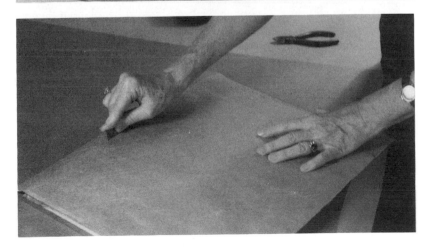

Fig. 5-15. *Trim off excess paper with a razor blade.*

Several mat samples were held against the print, and a plain white mat was selected. As this is a relatively small print, a 1½-inch mat will do. This makes the rabbet dimensions 9⅜ × 7⅛ inches. Choose a simple framer's molding. This style frame goes well with any print or photograph. The design of the molding works well for a learning project. It is easy to work with as the square sides fit snugly into a miter box.

Measuring the Molding

To figure the amount of wood to buy to make this frame, take these three things into consideration:

1. The width of the framer's molding. To figure waste wood, multiply the width of the molding (¾ inches) times the eight cuts needed to form the miters: 8 × ¾ inches = ²⁴⁄₄ inches = 3 inches.
2. Add the lengths of the four sides: 7⅛ inches + 7⅛ inches + 9⅜ inches + 9⅜ inches = 34 inches.
3. Add 1 inch for the displacement of the saw cuts. This is figured by adding the width of the cut (estimated at ⅛ inch) and multiplying it by the eight cuts: 8 × ⅛ inch = 1 inch.

You will need 3 inches + 34½ inches + 1 inch = 38½ inches of wood to complete your frame. If you could buy 4 feet of framer's molding that is all you would need. Most distributors, however, sell it in specific lengths of 6, 8, or 10 feet. At this stage of your experience, it might be wise to have extra wood, just in case you make an error in measuring or sawing. Also, this is a very versatile type of molding and can be used for other projects. Be careful how you store the wood before you cut your frame as well as any leftover wood. Don't stand it on end. Lay it flat against a dry wall. For this particular project, use a very soft wood that is easily cut in any miter box.

1. Before you use your miter box, be sure to place a piece of scrap lumber securely in the bottom to ensure a clean cut through the molding with no feathered edges.
2. Clamp your miter box in position. Cut your first piece of waste wood from either end. This is the first angled cut for the first long side of the frame.
3. Measure and mark 9⅜ inches to complete the first long side. Double check your figures and your mark before cutting. (Remember to cut the two long sides first so that any mistakes can end up as a shorter side.) Use a spring clamp to hold the molding firmly in place. With these short, thin lengths, you should have no trouble holding the wood in position while sawing, unless your first piece is cut from an 8-foot length. If that is the case, make sure you have someone help you, at least with the first few cuts.

Fig. 5-16. *Use an awl to start the hole for the screw eyes.*

Fig. 5-17. *The four sides of the frame, with waste pieces of wood.*

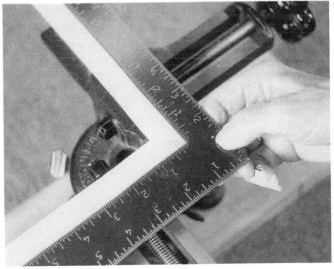

Fig. 5-18. *Miter vise with corner of framer's molding being joined.*

Fig. 5-19. *Examine the framer's molding for squareness.*

4. After cutting your two longer sides, cut the two shorter ones. Be sure to reverse the saw as you cut. In addition to the first piece of waste wood, you will have four more—assuming the frame is cut from one length of wood (Fig. 5-17).

Joining and Mitering the Frame

Some framers can glue and nail a mitered corner using a regular bench vise. Unless you possess mystical powers, don't try it. It is not easy. Easy is using a miter vise or corner clamps.

1. To check your work prior to joining, place each corner in a corner clamp or your miter vise to see if it forms a perfect miter. Juggle the long sides and short sides around until you find your best fit. They should meet almost perfectly. Again, set a work pattern for yourself: place a long side parallel to your body and the short side out from it in the miter vise (Fig. 5-18).

2. Adjust, glue, and nail. Use the nail set. Remember to put the wood glue on both pieces, so that a hairline escapes as you tighten it in the corner clamp or miter vise. (Wipe this glue away immediately with a damp cloth.)

3. Repeat with the other long and short side. Then, unite the two pieces. Check with your metal square to be certain of a perfect fit (Fig. 5-19).

4. Before you cut your mat, apply the finish to your frame. Set it aside.

5. Measure your finished frame. See if your original measurements still hold up. If you are slightly off, change the dimensions to accommodate this slight difference.

6. In keeping with "cut the most expendable items first," cut the backing board. With this fitted into position, you can be certain that you can go ahead and cut your mat, glass, and filler material to this same size.

☞ If the backing board has to be forced to fit, it is too tight. You will have trouble later when you cut your glass and mats to this size as they will have no room to expand. Trim the board down so you have at least ⅛ inch all around the frame for expansion for the paper and glass.

Cutting the Window Mat

Wash your hands before cutting the mat. Handle the mat carefully so oils from your hands do not transfer to the mat.

To demonstrate various cutters, a Dexter cutter is used here. The Dexter is the only cutter we know that cuts from the front. Other

Fig. 5-20. *Finish the second vertical cut with a Dexter cutter. Small dots on the mat act as cutting guidelines. Cut from the front. Keep the mat as free of marks as possible.*

Fig. 5-21. *Position the cut mat over the print.*

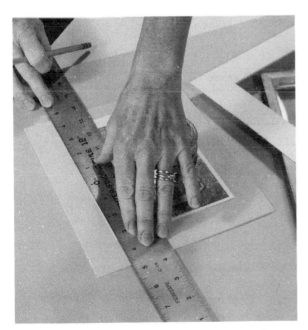

Fig. 5-22. *Rule the area of backboard to know where to reposition print for adhesive mounting. Ruled lines are drawn from edge to edge on all four sides to act as guidelines for positioning print.*

Fig. 5-23. *The completed project.*

brand-name cutters will be used in subsequent projects. You will cut a single mat.

1. With a ruler, place four tiny dots at the four corners on the front of your mat board where you want to cut the window.

2. Place the mat face up on a piece of scrap mat board. (Remember, the scrap board acts as a slip sheet and provides the extra area your blade needs to cut through the mat board yet not touch another hard surface.)

3. Clamp a straightedge to your working area, lining it up with two of your dots. Insert the blade firmly into the first lower dot, while your other hand holds the straightedge that will be your cutting guide. With your hand, grasp the cutter and push up ahead of you to the top dot (Fig. 5-20).

4. Repeat the process, carefully, remembering that you are working on the face of the mat. Move the slip sheet each time you make a cut, so that you do not wreck your mat by accidentally letting the blade fall back into a previously cut slot.

5. Test your window by positioning it over the artwork (Fig. 5-21) to be sure it is properly covered.

6. Place the print on a backing board, then take a ruler and draw a line around it (Fig. 5-22), with the four lines overlapping for easy replacement once you have applied mounting glue. Put a dab of white glue on the back of the artwork in the areas of the four corners and replace the print in position between the ruled lines on the backing board.

7. Cut a filler board to the size of your backing board. Place it under a clean piece of glass, lining up two sides of the filler board with the edges of the glass, and mark the other two sides for cutting. Use a felt-tipped pen or marker.

8. With your glass cutter, score the marked line and snap the glass off.

9. Check your glass for fingerprints and flaws. If it is okay, assemble glass, mat, artwork, and filler board. Add the dust cover, screw eyes, and wire. Figure 5-23 shows the completed project.

6:

CONSERVATION FRAMING

Everyone concerned with art is also concerned with conservation framing. There are already reams written on the natural enemies of paper—cold weather dryness, hot weather dampness, insects, pollution, dust, and light; as well as human enemies—mistakes in handling artwork and documents by selecting the wrong glue or backing paper or using paper products that contain acid.

CONSERVATION PRACTICES

This is not another book on conservation, and we will not dwell on the subject. You should have a basic understanding of its current importance in framing, however, and be aware of conservation practices. This widespread interest is relatively new. When bad framing practices are discovered, it isn't entirely fair to put the blame on the earlier framers. At the time, they did what they thought was right. The availability and knowledge of how to use conservation methods is something that only started about 10 years ago.

The following chapters will refer to conservation materials in step-by-step instructions for projects, when applicable. Realistically, some of the items being framed do not need or deserve the attention or expense of conservation materials. You should know they are available, however, in case you are framing anything that has sentimental value, is signed by an artist, or is a document or diploma. Frame these to conservation standards.

Things that you should never use when framing to conservation standards are pressure-sensitive tapes, masking tape, dry mounting, gummed brown tape, rubber cement, synthetic glue, regular corrugated backing board, or backing paper that has not been recommended for conservation use. You should use acid-free mats, boards, and backing paper.

When you purchase material for conservation framing, store it so it will not come in contact with material that could contaminate it and diminish its effectiveness. For instance, do not store conservation material in regular corrugated packing boxes; store them in special storage boxes.

If you encounter artwork or photographs that have been damaged, try to halt any further damage by rematting and reframing using conservation methods. Chapter 16 will show a few, simple, step-by-step procedures for reframing old photographs, etchings, and rubbings.

A DEGREE OF RESPECT

One example that needs conservation methods is if you are framing a degree from a college or university. If the person who has the diploma tells you to use cheaper methods, don't do it. Years from now, it's you who will get the blame if acid stain or mold gets on it. Suggest that after investing over $45,000 for that piece of paper, it should be treated with some respect and consideration.

The photograph in Fig. 6-1 shows a diploma that was framed with state-of-the-art conservation methods. It is hinged with Japanese hinges to a 100 percent rag backing board. (Japanese hinges are detailed in Chapter 7.) The backing board on the diploma is hinged with conservation quality linen tape to a 100 percent rag window mat. The hinging procedure

Fig. 6-1. *The diploma was framed using state-of-the-art conservation methods.*

68

is demonstrated in Chapter 3, Figs. 3-1 and 3-2. Filler board of rag was placed behind the mat when the frame was closed.

The subject of conservation framing is relatively new. The understanding of conservation should be a continuous learning process for all of us.

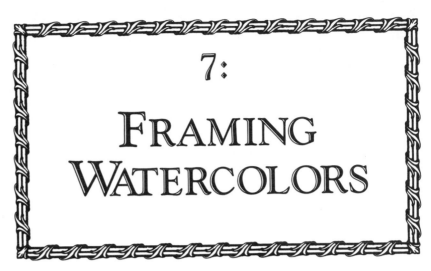

7:

FRAMING WATERCOLORS

In addition to the basic tools and materials listed in Chapter 5, the following items are used in framing watercolors:

Materials	Tools
adhesives (ATG gun, Sobo glue, removable transparent tape, wheat starch paste) • 100% rag mat board • foam core • pH neutral corrugated board • blotters • conservation hinges and linen tape • Japanese hinges	artist's paint brush • hair dryer • palette knife • paper weights

In framing watercolors, several considerations will affect the choices of mats and frames. If you are doing it for someone's home, you must know where it will hang and what the owner's framing and color preferences are. If an artist wants a work framed for possible exhibition, a basic white or off-white mat and a metal frame is best. If it will be shipped to various shows, you will want to use Plexiglas. (Many shippers will not accept glass.)

A WATERCOLOR PAINTING

Figure 7-1 shows Barbara Nechis with her painting that was used for the cover art of her book, *The Creative Experience*. When asked how she would like her art framed, the artist wanted an off-white rag mat and a blond contemporary oak frame. For this project, state-of-the-art conservation standards will be used throughout. A double-rag mat will be cut the same way as the one used in the Hopper project in

Chapter 5, with a few minor adjustments. Because no pencil markings should be used on rag board, all measurements will be made on Scotch 811 Tape (removable tape). By using this tape to mark all cutting lines, the mats can be cut without ever marking directly on them. This includes the slash mark on the first mat, the 5-inch mark for the bottom (Fig. 7-2), and the 4-inch measurements for the top and sides. A ¼-inch overlap of the painting is included in these measurements.

After cutting the first mat and checking for flaws, replace the dropout and remove the tape. Apply white glue around the window mat as well as a small amount on the center of the dropout to hold the second mat in position while it is being cut. Place new marks (again on removable tape) on the second mat and add ¼-inch marks all the way around to the original measurements. This shows where the liner, or second mat, is to be cut. After cutting the mats, remove the tape. Now hinge the window mat with linen tape to the four-ply rag backing board. Insta-Hinges, commercially made Japanese hinges, are used to attach the painting to the backing board in the example.

Insta-Hinge is a conservation mounting system that is both a gentle and a strong hinge. It has conservation paste already impregnated into the pretorn Japanese paper. All you do is add water, weight the hinges, and let dry. (Complete directions come with the package.) To meet conservation standards, this hinging process is removable with water.

Place the watercolor painting face down on the backing board. Dampen approximately ¼ inch on one end of the hinge with water and apply it to the painting (Fig. 7-3). Place blotters over the damp hinge (also Fig. 7-3) and paperweights on top of these; let the hinges dry. Turn the painting face up on the backing board. Position the window mat over the artwork to check the exact placement (Fig. 7-4) and apply the cross-tab hinges, crossing the T over the vertical hinges already on the artwork. Again, place weights over the hinges (Fig. 7-5). After

Fig. 7-1. *Barbara Nechis with her framed watercolor.*

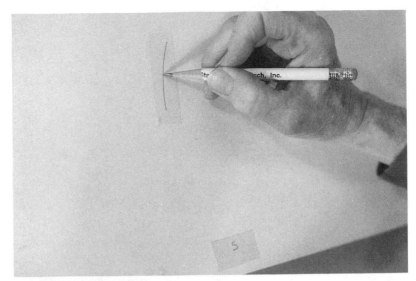

Fig. 7-2. *Use removable tape so no pencil marks are made directly on "museum-quality" boards.*

Fig. 7-3. *Insta-Hinges are for conservation mounting on reverse of watercolor.*

Fig. 7-4. *Position the artwork under the mat. Preliminary hinges are already in place on the back of the painting.*

Fig. 7-5. *Apply cross-tabs applied over vertical hinges, and place weights placed over the hinges until they are firm.*

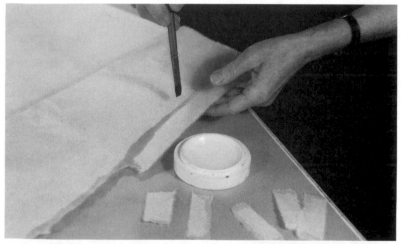

Fig. 7-6. *Paint a water line to soften Japanese paper.*

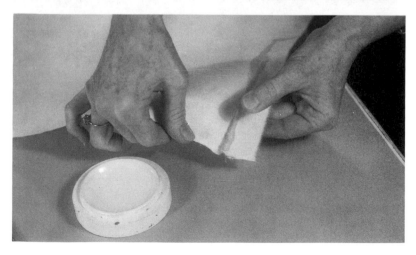

Fig. 7-7. *Tear a hinge of Japanese mulberry paper.*

the hinges are dry and firmly set, cut the glass for the frame. Place the mats and artwork on the glass, face down. Cut a filler board of acid-free foam core. Combine all these elements into the frame and close it.

FLOATING ARTWORK

For this project—framing Diane Etienne Faxon's watercolor, *Lincoln Autumn*—conservation methods are used again. The painting is designed to include the deckled edges of the paper, making it desirable to have the entire painting in the sight measurement. This means the artwork must *float*. A double mat can keep the painting from touching the glazing. Because this work might be entered in competition or exhibited in some manner, we selected white matting and placed it under Plexiglas in a metal frame, to withstand shipment and multiple handling.

One of the museum or conservation methods used included *mulberry hinges*, a Japanese paper hinge, to attach the painting to the backing board. Wheat starch paste is the adhesive used to hold the hinges. In keeping with all conservation practices, these are completely removable using water. Because this painting was done on Fabriano 140-pound paper (a medium-weight watercolor paper), select hinges that are slightly lighter in weight than the paper used for the artwork. Hinges are meant to hold a painting in place, but should the artwork be subjected to rough handling, it is the hinges that should tear and let go, not the paper the artwork is on. If the hinge is too strong, it is likely to tear the artwork instead.

To make these hinges, use a regular artist's brush, dipped in water, and "paint" a line on the Japanese paper (Fig. 7-6) to the length and width needed for the hinges. Then, gently tear the paper apart (Fig. 7-7) where the water has softened it. Tear. Never cut. The torn feathered edges will not show through to the face of the artwork. Straight cut edges often do show, especially if the art has been done on very lightweight paper.

With the Faxon artwork, four sets of hinges are used. The up-and-down strips are approximately 4 inches long, and the cross-hinges 2 inches. We cut a double mat from 100 percent rag mat board, allowing 1 inch of white space all around between the second or liner mat and the painting. A full-sized backing board of four-ply, 100 percent rag was also cut. To hold the artwork and permit it to float, the 4-inch, S-type hinges go through slots cut in the backing board and are firmly attached to the back side with 2-inch cross-hinges. Figure 7-8 is a cutaway illustration showing the process of floating art.

First, place the painting in position, with the double mat allowing a 1-inch space all around (Fig. 7-9). Note that removable tape outlines the top of the painting on the backing board. The pencil markings

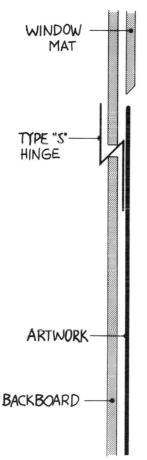

WINDOW MAT

TYPE "S" HINGE

ARTWORK

BACKBOARD

Fig. 7-8. *Diagram shows how to float art by hinging it through a slot in the backing board.*

are made on the tape for higher visibility. These marks also indicate where to place the four hinges as well as where to replace the artwork.

Turn the painting over and place the 4-inch-long Japanese hinges on the back of the artwork (Fig. 7-10). Align these carefully with the marks on the removable tape on the backing board. Then, using an artist's brush, dab wheat paste on ¼ inch of the end of the hinge that will be attached to the back of the painting (Fig. 7-11).

After the hinges dry, turn the painting over and reposition it using the marked tape as a guide. With a utility knife, cut slits in the backing board through the marks on the removable tape (Fig. 7-12). With a palette knife (Fig. 7-13) push each Japanese hinge through a slot in the backing board. Turn the backing board over carefully, with the painting held in place, and attach each cross-hinge to the long hinges (Fig. 7-14).

When the hinges are dry, inspect the artwork and mats to be sure that no dust, lint, or other foreign matter have become lodged on the mats or art. Conservation quality mat board has an amazing affinity for static electric attraction (Fig. 7-15). Figure 7-16 shows the framed, floating *Lincoln Autumn,* with the artist Diane Etienne Faxon, in her studio.

☞ If you find it difficult to remove masking tape, use a hair dryer. Heat softens the masking tape, and you can then pull it off—but do it gently.

The painting in Fig. 7-17 was done on 300-pound D'Arches paper, which is very heavy. In earlier projects, we have shown how linen tape can be used to hinge the window mat to a backing board. In this case, it is being used to hinge the painting directly to the backing board. This board is corrugated, but it is a special pH neutral corrugated.

Some hinge their artwork directly to a window mat because it is a simpler method to position it this way. The recommended way is to hinge the art to the much stronger backing board. If you hinge

Fig. 7-9. *Measure the 1 inch of white space to frame floating art. Make your marks on removable tape.*

heavy artwork to a weaker window mat, the latter could buckle under the weight. The linen hinge shown in Fig. 7-17 will be used to tape the painting to the backboard.

After the painting is placed in its metal frame, there is still space between the backing board and the frame. This can be filled with scrap mat board (Fig. 7-18). Use strips of mat board instead of springs to hold the package tight. Avoid using metal springs as they can literally "spring" out at you if the frame is picked up wrong. When trying to remove the artwork, a too-tight spring can also sometimes cause the glass to break. These scrap mat board spacers are literally free and do a better job; there is no need to ever use springs.

Figure 7-19 shows the artist Joan Scholtes with her finished watercolor, *Purple Majesty*. The watercolor is taped to the backboard and tightened with scrap mat board.

Figure 7-20 shows Filmoplast SH, (an easy-to-use, self-adhesive, white linen, pressure-sensitive tape) being used on another painting that was done on relatively heavy paper. It is being hinged to ³⁄₁₆-inch foam core—a lightweight but very firm backing. In this case, it became both backing and filler board because of its thickness.

A large double mat was used on this painting. As added protection, a dab of Sobo white glue placed under the edge of the liner helps keep the mats securely in place (Fig. 7-21). Figure 7-22 shows Donna Shuford's

Fig. 7-10. *Use marks on tape to line up the hinges.*

Fig. 7-11. *Dab wheat paste onto ¼ inch of the hinge.*

Fig. 7-12. *Turn the painting over and reposition, using removable tape marks as a guide for slitting areas for the hinges to be inserted.*

Fig. 7-13. *Palette knife pushing 4-inch hinge through slot.*

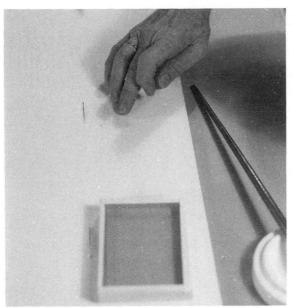

Fig. 7-14. *Attach a cross hinge. Foreground shows a weight on the first completed hinge. Background shows the next hinge to be fastened.*

Fig. 7-15. *Check for dust and lint. Rag mat has a particular affinity for attracting dust from the area.*

Fig. 7-16. *Diane Etienne Faxon's watercolor,* Lincoln Autumn, *floating in its new frame in her studio.*

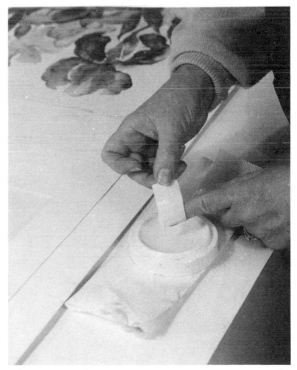

Fig. 7-17. *A linen hinge has adhesive that becomes active when dipped in water; it is being applied to pH neutral board.*

painting, *Fracturing Forces*, before being inserted into a metal frame.

The paintings by Scholtes and Shuford just discussed are typical of the way artists frame and exhibit their work today in what could be called "in-and-out" frames. None of the framing is done with state-of-the-art standards in mind. The artist generally uses regular, rather than rag, mat board and linen or pressure-sensitive tape to hinge the artwork to the backing boards. In this way, the painting can be removed, still attached to its backing board, and another piece of artwork easily inserted into that same frame, and on to the next show.

Fig. 7-18. *Fill the space between the backing board and the metal frame with strips of mat board—an efficient and inexpensive process.*

Fig. 7-19. *Artist Joan Scholtes next to her framed watercolor.* Purple Majesty.

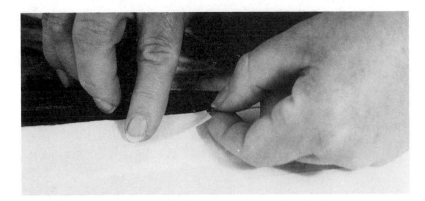

Fig. 7-20. *Hinging with Filmoplast SH. After the hinge is applied, it must be burnished.*

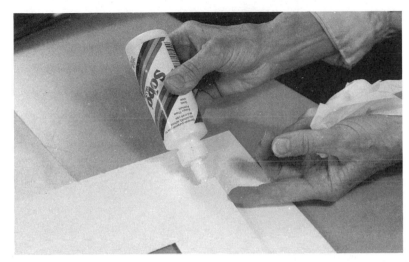

Fig. 7-21. *Apply white glue under the edges of the liner mat for added strength.*

Fig. 7-22. *Donna Shuford's Fracturing Forces is ready to be inserted in a metal frame.*

8:

FRAMING
OILS

In addition to the basic tools and materials listed in Chapter 5, the following items are used in framing oils:

Materials

Adhesives (Scotch Spray Adhesive 77, 811 Scotch Brand Magic Plus removable tape • wood glue • fabric • finishing materials (Butcher's wax, Rub 'n Buff ebony, tung oil) • foam core • hardware (mending plates, offset clips, screw eyes, wire) • kraft paper • wood (corner and framer's molding, insert molding, lathe strips, parting strips)

Tools

awl • burnishing bone • razor blade • staple gun

In framing oils, you probably will not want to use glass. If you are planning on entering an oil or acrylic in competition, you cannot use glass in juried shows. You might want to use an insert liner between the canvas and the frame. This insert is often fabric covered, but not always. With an oil painting, the insert serves much the same purpose as a mat with a photograph or watercolor or print: it enhances and protects while providing the necessary breathing space.

Today's artists tend to shy away from elaborate decorative framing for their oils. They often use thin strips of wood around the canvas. Builder's corner molding also provides a good frame for holding oils. This is not to say there is no place for more elaborate frames. It depends upon the subject matter of the painting, the style, and the personal preferences of the artist or owner of the work.

We will show you how to fit an oil painting into basic frames and how to make the insert. These same techniques can work with any style frame, simple or elaborate.

FRAMING A STUDENT OIL PAINTED ON CANVAS BOARD

The first considerations in framing student oils is that they be framed inexpensively and be properly wired for hanging in a show. One favorite solution is to use corner molding, sold in lumberyards in some sections of the country as carpenter's molding. It forms a frame that the painting literally rests on, while being protected on all sides.

Fig. 8-1. *Spread glue on the inside back edges. For convenience, pour a small amount of glue onto a mat board scrap.*

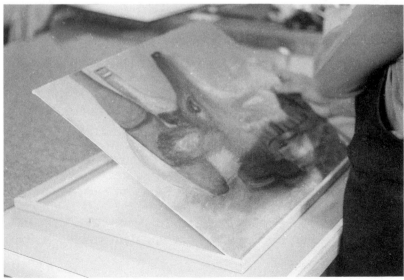

Fig. 8-2. *Place the back side of the oil painting onto the glue.*

84

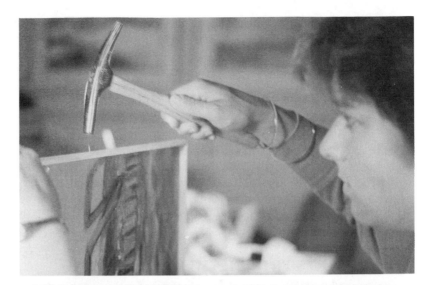

Fig. 8-3. *Small brads hold the oil and frame together.*

Fig. 8-4. *Attach eye screws and wire to the back of the frame.*

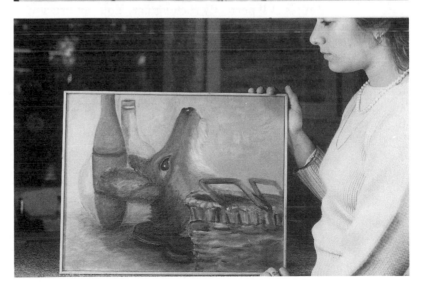

Fig. 8-5. *The framed oil,* Still Life, *and artist Alicia Bannon.*

This type of molding fits neatly into the miter box as it has a perfect right-angle design, which makes it easy to handle while cutting. When the frame is completed, turn it over. What is normally the front of the frame becomes the back for oils, where the canvas board will be mounted. After the corners have been nailed and glued, more glue is daubed on the inside back (Fig. 8-1) of the frame to hold the mounted canvas.

Figure 8-2 shows the oil being placed into the frame. Nails (Fig. 8-3) are carefully driven through the frame into the side of the board, and screw eyes and wire are added (Fig. 8-4). Rubbing tung oil (a wood finish) on with a soft cloth and wiping clean gives the wood a very nice finish. Butcher's wax (a household paste wax) is then rubbed on and off later to give added luster and protection. The completed frame is shown in Fig. 8-5.

WOOD STRIP FRAMING: STRIPPING

Another good framing material for oils is wood lathing—thin narrow strips of wood similar in size to that used in trellises, but of a better grade. The example being framed here is another student oil that will be entered in competition. The canvas was stapled to the stretcher before the oil was painted. The frame edges will be butted together rather than using mitered corners, as you would with more decorative framing material. You use straight, right-angle cuts for this, using the 90-degree guide of your miter box, or you can simply have the lumberyard cut them to size.

Figure 8-6 is a diagram of how the four pieces of stripping are positioned for nailing. Before you do the nailing, check your work by placing the four strips against the stretched canvas to make sure the painting will fit snugly within this frame. (Also check to make sure your painting is still perfectly rectangular. You can use a metal square or measure the two diagonal directions—if they are exactly the same, it is squared off.) Figure 8-7 shows one of the lathing wood corners being nailed, after the areas to be butted and nailed have been daubed with wood glue for added strength. Before the glue on the fourth corner has a chance to set, place the painting inside the frame and pull the corners together against the sides of the canvas. Nail the final corner.

☞ Many artists nail the lathing directly into the sides of the stretcher, without gluing. The use of lathing is a temporary measure and not considered a permanent frame.

This frame is not designed to take a rabbet, so it must be attached firmly to the canvas and the stretcher with nails (Fig. 8-8), two to three per side. Instead of a dust cover, place foam core on the back. Punch air holes in the foam core first, using an awl (Fig. 8-9). Oils

C-1. This Monet shows that with different approaches to matting and framing, subtle things happen. Decide which mats enhance your print.

C-2. Different mat combinations will pick up different colors in this watercolor. Different widths of inner mats also produce different effects. *(bottom)* Several shades of red show different effects.

C-3. *(top)* A variety of mat and frame combinations, including samples of reverse bevel cuts and black-core double mats, are shown. Because the print is of some value, all the mats are acid-free. *(bottom)* Different colors of mats can also enhance groupings. Acid-free material is again used for these original watercolors.

C-4. Wooden frames are available in a variety of finishes and designs, from the simplest profile to ornate gold leaf and built-up designs.

C-5. *(top)* You can find high-lacquer finishes for frames in a variety of colors. *(bottom)* This series of frames features graduated sizes from ½ to 1½ inches, and includes moldings with linen liners and deep rabbets to accommodate oil paintings stretched on canvas.

C-6. *(top)* Paper mats in a variety of color combinations. *(bottom)* Textured mats, from left to right: cork, linen, reverse bevel, silk, and suede.

C-7. *(top)* This series of wooden frames features painted finishes in different sizes and families of color combinations. *(bottom)* A variety of metal frames (courtesy of American Frame Corp.).

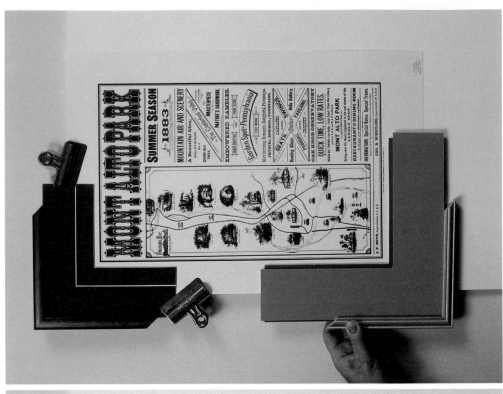

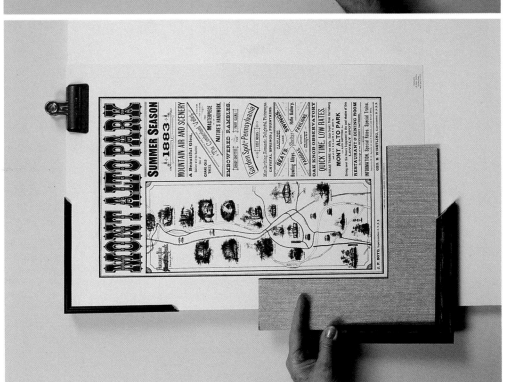

C-8. You could frame this poster with or without a mat. You also can choose a variety of mat types, including reverse bevel and double mats.

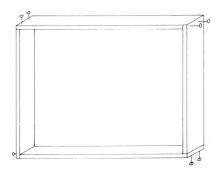

Lathing, Used as Frame Around Oil

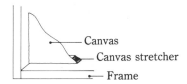

Canvas
Canvas stretcher
Frame

Front face of canvas
is recessed slightly

Fig. 8-6. *Diagram shows how to position and nail the wood strips around the painting.*

need up to three years to dry thoroughly, and these holes provide the necessary ventilation for circulation during this time. The foam core protects the canvas from being damaged should it be stacked against other paintings while waiting to be exhibited or if it is roughly handled during shipping. The backing also keeps dust, dirt, insects, and other foreign matter out of the back of the frame. With the addition of screw eyes and wire, the frame is completed. Normally you would not screw any hardware material directly into a stretcher frame, but with this thin stripping, it is necessary.

FABRIC-WRAPPED INSERTS

The oil painting used in this example was purchased on a recent trip to Spain (Fig. 8-10). It will be framed, perhaps not with all the care that would go into the framing of a painting that is considered a major investment, but in a way that will last for generations, if not posterity. The fabric insert, which you will learn how to make, is done using the same techniques that you would use on more expensive frames. In this case, the right way is the only way.

This Spanish oil is relatively small and lightweight and was purchased unmounted. Because it needed a support, one was made of parting strip wood. Figure 8-11 shows the oil being pulled over this support bar, ready for stapling. Next, measure the outside of the stretched oil to get the dimensions for the insert. Be sure to allow for the folds made as the canvas is wrapped around the corners of the support as there must be room to fit it in the rabbet.

Fig. 8-7. *(top left) Nailing a corner that has been glued first.*

Fig. 8-8. *(top right) Drive nails into the canvas and stretcher.*

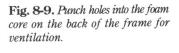

Fig. 8-9. *Punch holes into the foam core on the back of the frame for ventilation.*

Fig. 8-10. *Oil painting with the parting-strip support form and cloth-covered insert. Use a staple gun to attach oil to the support.*

Fig. 8-11. *Getting ready to insert third staple in center of top. Note staple in center on side of frame. Work out from these center staples when attaching painting.*

☞ To frame a more valuable oil painting, use stretcher bars. The sloped face of a stretcher bar will keep the canvas from resting directly on the wood face.

For this insert frame, special framer's molding was purchased. It has a simple convex design, variations of which are used for most wrapped fabric inserts. Cut the molding the same as you would for any framer's molding frame. The next step is to wrap each piece of this molding. You will find this useful with many types of frames.

Cloth-covered wood molding makes a beautiful liner or insert for oils as well as for other types of framing. Again, it is easy to do, and once you learn the process, you will find many ways to use it. The most obvious is to make your own linen-wrapped inserts that will separate the painting from the wood frame.

Choose wood molding with simple covings or quarter-round type designs. You must be sure that the cloth adheres properly to the surface, and these are the easiest to work with.

As an *insert* is a frame within a frame, remember that you need a rabbet on the insert, just as you do on any frame (Fig. 8-12). If you use a builder's molding (a 1-inch wide version of the wood used in the Hopper project, for example) you will also need a parting strip to form the rabbet.

☞ A good way to practice wrapping cloth on insert molding is to take a facial tissue and wrap it around the mitered corner and rabbet areas of your molding. Doing this will show you how you need to fold and cut to make a smooth mitered corner.

89

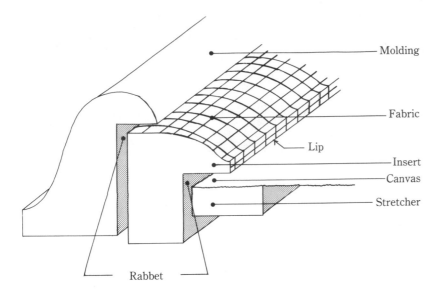

Molding

Fabric

Lip

Insert

Canvas

Stretcher

Rabbet

Fig. 8-12. *Cutaway illustration showing how insert frame fits into rabbet of regular frame.*

At this point, it is assumed that you have measured and cut your wood insert strips. To cover them with fabric:

1. Cut four strips of fabric. For this first project, cut them one at a time. If you goof, you might as well goof as inexpensively as possible. Place your first strip of insert wood down on a piece of the uncut cloth to measure how much you will need; that is, enough to cover the top part of the rabbet and enough to cover the face (the part that will be seen) of the insert wood. The back part of your insert will be covered by the overlapping rabbet that is part of the basic frame. This frame will hold the insert as well as the stretched canvas (see Fig. 8-12 again). Cut the cloth so that it is about 2 inches longer than the insert wood (1 inch on both ends), or just wide enough to cover the face and upper part of the rabbet and long enough to fold into the mitered cut areas.

2. Spray adhesive (or brush on glue, whichever you prefer) on the back of the fabric.

☞ To hold the fabric in your spray box, put removable scotch tape on both ends (Fig. 8-13) and tape the strip vertically in the spraying area. You will be able to hold the sticky cloth easier with these "handles," after the cloth has been sprayed.

3. Place the sprayed fabric face down. Position the wood (Fig. 8-14) before the glue sets. With a thin, but blunt, instrument (Fig. 8-15) and your fingers, work the cloth into the upper portion of the rabbet. If you have gooey glue, be careful that it does not seep through onto the face of the fabric. (If it does, you are either pressing too hard or using too much glue. If you have sprayed the fabric, rather than daubed the glue on, you should not have any trouble with this.) Work fabric against wood until it sticks evenly over the face. Start with the rabbet and work up and around. Use the palm of your hand. The fabric should be perfectly flat against the wood with no wrinkles.

4. With a razor blade or utility knife, trim excess cloth away. Start with the mitered corners before the glue has a chance to set, pulling the cloth as tight as you can onto the mitered surface. With your razor, cut small triangle shapes (Fig. 8-16) out of the cloth as you work it firmly against or onto the mitered area. (You are going to glue and nail these corners to form your insert, just as you would with a regular wood frame miter.) With a little practice, you will be able to do this perfectly. Try it three times on scrap before you do the real thing, and remember our suggestion to practice using tissue. Once you have your mitered areas wrapped, with no cloth lumps, trim the other excess material away. Start where the 90-degree angle hits in the rabbet notch (Fig. 8-17). Trim the back side of the insert (Fig. 8-18).

5. Repeat the process and wrap the other three sides (Fig. 8-19). Place one long side in your miter vise with one of the shorter sides. If you have worked the cloth properly, you should get a perfect seam for your corner. Apply regular wood glue and nail the corner as you have done on other frames.

6. Join the other two sides, then join your frame.

The insert is now completed and ready to be placed around the Spanish oil. Fit the insert snugly around the canvas and its support, but not so tightly that there is no give at all. If you have to force it, it is too tight. Hold the oil and the insert together with offset clips (Fig. 8-20) that screw into the insert and hold the support bars. This hardware is available in various sizes for frames.

We cut the frame from a swan-shaped framer's molding. It was difficult to get perfect miters with this molding because it would not easily hold flat in the miter box. Once we got it together, however, it made a beautiful frame, finished with a Rub 'n Buff ebony. The fabric insert that holds the canvas and its support is in turn held in the outside frame with brass mending plates (see Fig. 8-20). The canvas has a protective kraft dust cover and is placed on a living room wall.

HOW A PROFESSIONAL
OIL PAINTER FRAMES HER WORK

A professional oil painter almost always paints on canvas that has been stapled over stretcher bars. When the painting is completed, the decision is then made on how to frame it. The paintings must be

Fig. 8-13. *(top left) Removable tape makes handling of fabric easier after glue has been sprayed on the cloth.*

Fig. 8-14. *(top right) Position the insert wood over the fabric with adhesive sprayed over the back side of cloth.*

Fig. 8-15. *(middle left) Use a burnishing bone as blunt instrument to work fabric into rabbet area and other wood configurations.*

Fig. 8-16. *(middle right) Trim excess fabric from the insert with a razor blade.*

Fig. 8-17. *(bottom left) Trim the back side of the insert.*

Fig. 8-18. *Work fabric into mitered corners with your razor blade, cutting off small pieces a little at a time to get a flat corner that can be perfectly mitered.*

Fig. 8-19. *The other three sides of the fabric-wrapped insert.*

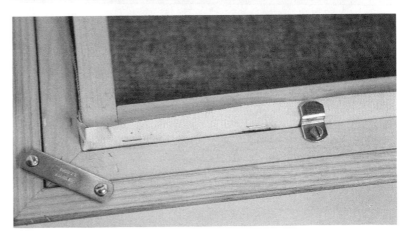

Fig. 8-20. *Fit the stretched canvas into the insert. Hold the canvas in position with offset clips. Fasten a screw into the insert to hold the clip.*

protected against rough handling and the danger of puncture when stacked against other paintings, because as movers and handlers pay little heed to whether they are handling a student's oil or a professional's livelihood. These problems exist and are magnified as the economic value of the paintings increase. In addition to backing, a painting can be recessed slightly so that the frame helps to protect the oil painting. In recessing, however, be careful not to set it back so far that shadows from the frame detract from the art.

Figure 8-21 shows Joan Heston, award-winning artist and former president of Allied Artists of America, Inc., in her studio in Connecticut. Here she keeps an assortment of sample pieces of framing that she can use to decide how a finished canvas will look with various types of framing wood (Fig. 8-22). She can place both flat and corner samples against a completed oil to see how more than one style will look, giving her a better idea of which is right for that particular painting.

For most of her oils, Heston prefers a simple frame with a spacer strip (Fig. 8-23) that is nailed directly into the frame. This strip is sometimes dark, sometimes light, depending upon the individual painting. In addition to the strip molding, she also uses carpenter's corner molding in reverse as a frame (Fig. 8-24). Heston prefers to have a narrow air space between canvas and frame when using this reverse frame technique. To get a proper fit, she has developed a system of using ¼-inch shims between the frame and the painting, which are removed once the canvas has been attached to the carpenter's corner molding (Fig. 8-25).

☞ When you use this type of frame, cover the staples or unfinished areas around the sides of your canvas with tape.

Fig. 8-21. *Artist Joan Heston checks framing samples for her oil painting,* Suzanne's Day.

Fig. 8-22. *Sampling corners with several different stains (identified on the edges of the sample). Inside of frame can be painted to complement colors in painting.*

Fig. 8-23. *Considering spacer strips with carpenter's corner molding.*

Fig. 8-24. *Carpenter's corner molding with air space between canvas and frame. The corner molding can be stained or painted gold or silver.*

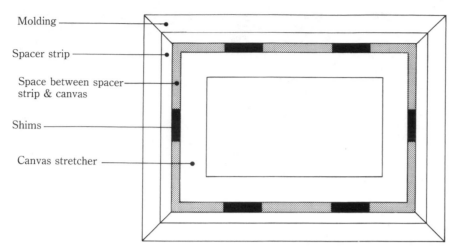

Molding

Spacer strip

Space between spacer
strip & canvas

Shims

Canvas stretcher

Fig. 8-25. *To position canvas in frame, place temporary shims between the canvas and spacer strips.*

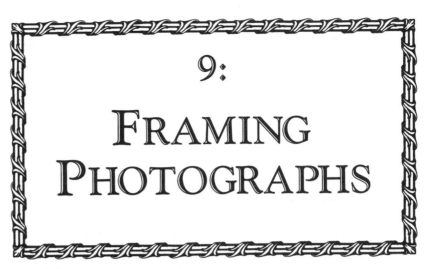

9:

FRAMING PHOTOGRAPHS

In addition to the basic tools and materials listed in Chapter 5, the following items are used in framing photographs:

Materials	Tools
mounting corners (clear archival)	white cotton gloves
• metal frame plus hardware	

Once you know how to cut a mat and put a frame together, you know how to frame a photograph. Many of the same rules you encounter in framing watercolors will apply when framing a photograph. You do not want glass to be directly against the print. If the framed photograph is subjected to humidity, this moisture will be trapped, and the print could stick to the glass.

In the examples in this chapter, we show you how to approach each project and how to choose specific matting and framing. Often framers settle for a simple metal frame or a thin wood framer's molding, which is fine. These projects show how, with a little imagination, you can enhance the print using different types of framing and finishes as well as interesting matting.

THE BASIC METAL FRAME

The photo used in this project was one that had been mounted on foam core and hung on a wall without a frame. Now it will be placed in a metal frame with a mat to protect it from the glass.

☞ Before you begin to assemble any metal frame, run a damp cloth or paper towel through the channels of the frame to get rid of any bits of dirt and dust.

Choose a double mat for your photo and hinge it to a backing board. (This operation is shown in Chapter 3 with the instructions on how to cut a double mat.) Buy a metal frame, cut to size. Figure 9-1 shows a close-up of how to assemble the hardware, and Fig. 9-2 shows how to put your metal frame together. The step-by-step procedure is:

   1. In Fig. 9-2, place one of the long pieces of framing hardware in front of you, front side down. Attach one short side to the long piece.

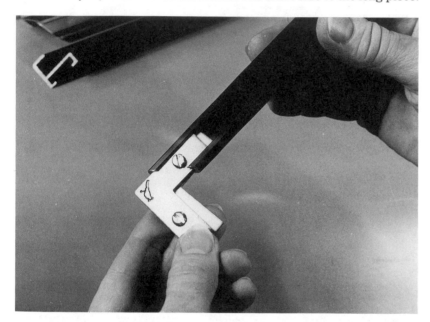

Fig. 9-1. *How the hardware goes into the channel of a metal frame.*

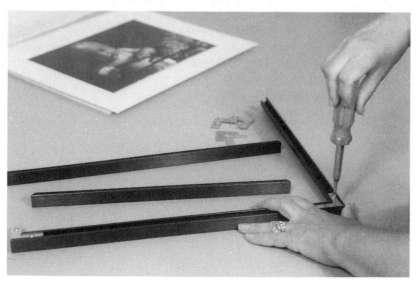

Fig. 9-2. *Join two sides and tighten the screws.*

2. Figure 9-2 also shows the hardware in one end of the long piece. This is joined to one of the short sides. Tighten the two screws.

3. Add the hardware to the other end of the long side, attaching it to the other short side. Tighten these screws.

4. Wash the glass. Place it face down on a firm, lint-free surface, such as an old army blanket or felt. Place the package of mat, photo, backing board, and filler board on top of the glass. Turn the glass and the rest of the package over. Check for dust. A chemically treated dusting cloth or a blast from an aerosol can of air will come in handy if there is any dust.

☞ When you are sliding the glass and package into the frame, brace the frame up against a wall or some solid object before slipping the package into position in the frame (Fig. 9-3).

5. Turn the frame face up. Slide the glass and the package into the channels of the frame (Fig. 9-3). Turn the frame over again and place the last pieces of hardware into the frame. These must be inserted at the same time, before you tighten either one (Fig. 9-4). Push together, then tighten.

6. Turn the frame around. See if the mitered corners look okay to you. If not, don't take it all apart; just loosen the screws and reposition.

☞ Another reason for placing the glass and the package face up (see Fig. 9-3 again) is that you are less likely to drag dust in with it when you push the package into the frame.

7. From the top, measure about one-third down the back of the frame to add your hangers. (*Note*: before you close up the frame, double check the type of metal frame you are using. Some must have the hangers added before you add the fourth side.) Add your hanging wire (Fig. 9-5), so that it arches up about halfway between the top of the frame and where you have placed your hangers.

FRAMING A HIGH-GLOSS COLOR PHOTO

The framing of original color photographs sometimes calls for special handling. Because some photographs tend to fade, you might have one that you want to exhibit for a short time, then put away. To demonstrate how to handle this, we are using *archival mounting corners*, which is one of the state-of-the-art methods available. These hold the photo in position on the backing board (Fig. 9-6). Because the directions on how to use these vary, follow the method suggested by the manufacturer of the brand you choose. The photo is inserted into the corners (Fig. 9-7) and then placed in the frame.

Fig. 9-3. *Brace the frame against a wall or solid object when inserting the entire assemblage: the glass, picture, mats, backing.*

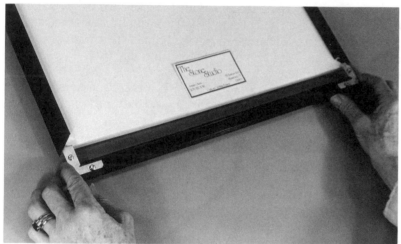

Fig. 9-4. *With most metal frames, both of the last two pieces of hardware must be inserted at the same time and in position on the final side before any of their screws are tightened.*

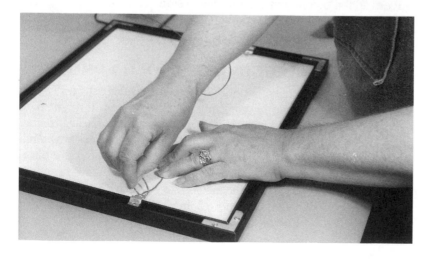

Fig. 9-5. *Place hangers and wire approximately one-third of the way down the back.*

☞ Note the cotton gloves used in handling this print. It is one way to make sure you do not get fingerprints on your work.

THE BASIC WOOD FRAME

Figure 9-8 shows an easy-to-make frame that is good to use, whether you are planning to exhibit your photograph or hang it in your home or office. The wood is a type that is found in both lumberyards and framing stores, with minor variations. Framer's molding categorizes it as a "flat." Some lumberyards identify it as "back band," grouping it with caps or corner moldings. It is very easy to cut and assemble.

The steel mill photograph was mounted to a backing board. The basic single mat was attached with linen tape to this backboard, as demonstrated in Chapter 3. The wood frame was sprayed matte black.

ADDING SOMETHING SPECIAL

With this snow scene photographed by Clyde W. Hare (Fig. 9-9), a double-bevel, forming a V groove, was cut into a special white mat with a black core. This enhances the picture without distracting from it. The process of cutting specialized decorative grooves is best left to an experienced mat cutter. It is another of the professional services that you should keep in mind for future projects. There are also special courses in this type of mat cutting, if you enjoy this branch of framing.

Fig. 9-6. *Archival mounting corners.*

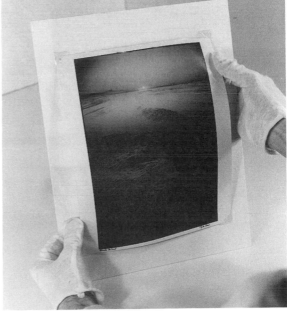

Fig. 9-7. *Photo being inserted into corners. Cotton gloves prevent fingerprints. (Photograph,* Bayless Island, *courtesy of photographer Clyde W. Hare.)*

The swan-shaped molding is oak. The finish is Rub 'n Buff ebony worked in with a soft cloth and fingers, then buffed to a high gloss.

TRIPLE FEATURE:
DISPLAYING SEVERAL PHOTOS IN ONE FRAME

An interesting way to mat and frame a group of photographs that have a relationship is to group them under one mat with multiple openings (Fig. 9-10). Once you have mastered the basics of cutting a regular mat, it is not at all difficult to cut a mat with one, two, or more openings.

To frame three photographs using one mat:

1. Start by placing the photos on a blank surface. Move them around until you like the way they go together and decide on an overall size.

2. You now know how you want them placed. You have decided to leave a 2-inch outer border. The vertical photo will be equidistant, top and bottom (Fig. 9-11).

3. Once you decide where you want your photos, flip your mat over and mark the areas to cut on the back. This means that you must repeat your layout, but in reverse.

4. Remember that the individual mat edges will overlap the photos to hold them and keep them from popping out of their windows. To help you lay out your reverse pattern, cut three pieces of scrap board

Fig. 9-8. *Builder's molding (back band) is ideal for framing photographs. (Photograph courtesy of Clyde W. Hare.)*

Fig. 9-9. *A V groove cut into a mat enhances the presentation of this photograph. (Photograph courtesy of Clyde W. Hare.)*

Fig. 9-10. Red's Woods *groups three photos under one mat. (Photograph courtesy of Clyde W. Hare.)*

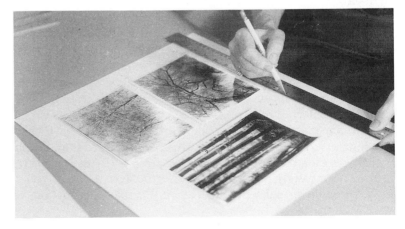

Fig. 9-11. *Measuring for placement of multiple grouping of photos.*

to the size of your window openings (remember that these openings will be approximately ⅛ inch smaller all around than the items you are matting). Use these as dummies to repeat your layout on the back of the mat (Fig. 9-12). This will help you mark your final cutting lines.

☞ Figure 9-13 shows an optional tool—a corner marker—that is very handy for this project. It is simple to use and saves time when measuring in two directions at once.

A second useful optional tool is a center-finding rule. As its name suggests, it helps you find the center of a photo or mat board almost instantly. The O mark indicates the center mark you are looking for, as long as you have the same measurement marks on both the right and left side of the O.

Figure 9-14 shows the guidelines being placed on the back of the mat. These show exactly where to insert the mat cutter. *Remember*: you are working in reverse of your original plan. You might feel we are overemphasizing this reminder, but we know professionals who have completed a multiple opening, mat cutting job, only to discover they ended up in reverse of their original design. Of course, they pretended that it was what they had planned all along!

Figure 9-15 shows how to rotate the mat when you cut the openings. You do not simply cut all the horizontal lines, and then all the vertical lines. If you do, you will have bevels going in on one side and out of the other. Figure 9-10 shows the completed job. It's just the way we planned it all along!

POSITIONABLE MOUNTING ADHESIVE (PMA)

PMA is an inexpensive method of mounting. It allows you to position and reposition your artwork until you are satisfied it is exactly where you want it. The adhesive comes in rolls of various sizes. You can use it with a wringer-type roller, or it can be burnished very easily by hand.

The photograph used in this project was taken in Guatemala, in 1965, and framed against the glass. It stuck there. The photo was unframed, and the glass with its stuck contents submerged in a Pyrex dish of water. (This does not always work, but we were lucky: the photo lifted right off.) Plastic-coated clips held it suspended until it was dry. Then, a sheet of adhesive mounting tissue was cut from the roll and transferred to the back of the dried photo (Fig. 9-16), using a wide, flat plastic tool that comes with the package of PMA.

Figure 9-17 shows the transfer paper being peeled from the photo, which was then placed on a backing board (Fig. 9-18). At this point, it is still completely positionable. Once you have it where you want it, just press firmly all over, and it stays. (Complete instructions come with the kit.)

Fig. 9-12. *Using dummy photographs can help you when you are setting up the reverse side of your mat for cutting window openings.*

Fig. 9-13. *A corner marker is an optional tool that helps you measure two directions at the same time.*

Fig. 9-14. *Mark the lines to cut openings from the back of the mat. Original layout is in the background as a guide.*

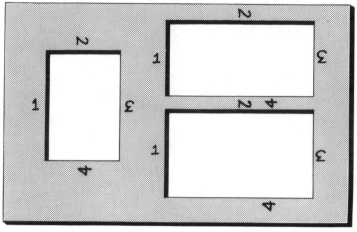

Mat with
Multiple
Openings

Fig. 9-15. *This rotation diagram shows the sequence in which you make your cuts.*

HOW TO TREAT A PHOTOGRAPH AS AN OIL

The photograph in Fig. 9-19 used in this project was texturized. It could then be treated as an oil painting and framed without glass. It was to hang in a child's room. The texturizing makes it completely scrubbable.

The texturizing was done in a dry-mount press using heat. There are several different texturizing finishes available (linen, matte, and others). We chose a texture that looks like brush strokes.

To frame the hare, we cut a mat from ³⁄₁₆-inch foam core and hand-wrapped it with velvet. (See Fig. 9-20. For instructions on hand wrapping mats, see Chapter 10.) The velvet was pulled tight against the bevel. The thick slope gives the picture added dimension.

The frame was an attic frame cut down to fit this photograph. We took it apart and removed about 1½ inches, then reassembled it as if it were a new frame.

Fig. 9-16. *A complete PMA kit. Transfer the adhesive from the sheet (cut from roll in foreground) to the back of the photo.*

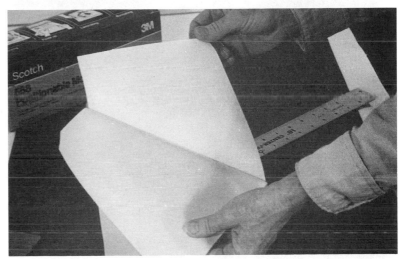

Fig. 9-17. *By using pressure, you transfer the adhesive from the tissue to the back of the photo, then peel off the transfer sheet.*

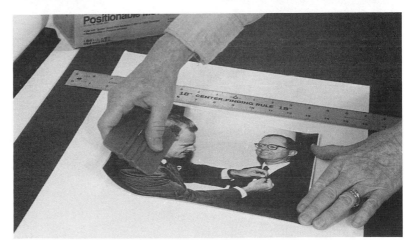

Fig. 9-18. *Position the photo on the backing board. Apply pressure to adhere the two together.*

Fig. 9-19. *The texturized rabbit. (Photo* Hare Today, Hare Tomorrow *by Gerald Hare.)*

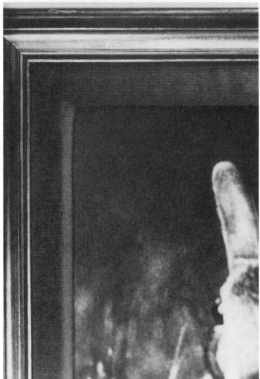

Fig. 9-20. *Close-up shows the velvet-covered foam core. This fabric-wrapped mat looks very much like the fabric-wrapped inserts used with oils.*

10:
FABRIC-WRAPPED MATS

In addition to the basic tools and materials listed in Chapter 5, the following items are used to make fabric-wrapped mats:

Materials	Tools
fabric • mat board • glue or spray adhesive • foam core	ATG gun • household iron • razor blade • rulers

An inexpensive way to add a look of elegance to a print, painting, or photograph is to use a fabric-wrapped mat. Buying these commercially can cost the proverbial arm and a leg, but it is relatively simple and inexpensive to wrap a mat.

Plan your project. Be sure you do not forget that frames and mats are meant to enhance—not call attention to themselves.

For your first covered mats, stay away from sheer fabrics as well as heavy, textured fabric that will be difficult to manipulate. Use a light-colored mat board. At least, do not use a dark mat board with light-colored material. Do not mark on the mat board if you are using a light color as these marks will probably show through. This is not to say that you cannot ever use sheer fabrics or bulky ones—just don't start with them. Use opaque and easy-to-handle fabrics at first. With a little practice, you will be able to use a wide variety of materials. "Practice" is the key word again. It will not take you long, but try the following procedures with scraps of fabric and mat board before you try working with the real thing.

WRAPPING YOUR MAT

Cut your mat from regular mat board. To do a full-size mat, cut the fabric slightly larger than the mat board. You will trim the outside to the same size as the board. (For liner mats, you can use less material, as less than an inch will normally show in the finished frame.)

Experiment with using the front of your mat as well as the back for gluing your fabric. Each way gives a slightly different result. When fabric is glued to the face of the mat, the bevel slopes into your artwork. If you turn the mat over, with the fabric on the back, the reverse bevel gives a sharper look. For the photograph of the rabbit in the child's room in the color section (grouped with the Monet prints), the fabric was mounted to foam core and slopes into the picture, giving an illusion of the type of insert associated with oil paintings. For the series in this chapter, the fabric is mounted to the backs of the mats.

The easiest way to cover your mat with adhesive is to use a spray. If you do, be careful of the fumes. Try to do it outside or have plenty of ventilation. Also, read your directions carefully. Line up the nozzle as directed. Start the spraying operation to one side of the object and bring the spray across the object and over. If you use glue on the front (or back, as you decide), use an ATG gun on the other side of the mat when you pull the fabric around and want to have it hold tight.

To wrap a mat:

1. Iron your fabric.

2. Cut your mat. Experiment to decide how you prefer the bevel to slope, then spray one side with adhesive or spread glue over the surface.

3. Place the mat, adhesive side down, on the back side of your ironed fabric. Pull the cloth taut as you can before placing the mat. If there are directional lines in the weave of the cloth, be sure you have them straight.

4. Check to be sure cloth and mat adhere smoothly. Trim the outside edges with a razor blade (Fig. 10-1).

5. Cut a square out of the center of the cloth, leaving an inch or so to wrap around to the back of your mat (Fig. 10-2).

☞ In cutting your square of fabric out of the center of the mat, use a steel ruler as a stop (see Fig. 10-2) to make sure you do not cut too far with your razor blade.

6. With your razor blade, cut a diagonal line from each corner out toward the center (Fig. 10-3). Do not cut right up to the corner of the mat board. Working from both the back and the front, use your razor blade to finish your diagonal cut while pulling the cloth taut to make sure you have it positioned where you want it. This is one area where practice really will make perfect. Try it with scrap, first, as you will probably fail at your first attempt to get a perfectly wrapped corner.

7. On the back side of the mat, place adhesive on the ½-inch area your cloth will cover (Fig. 10-4).

Fig. 10-1. *Trim the outside edge of the mat. Note that the first side on the right has already been trimmed.*

Fig. 10-2. *(above, left) Rulers provide a perfect stopping barrier when cutting center from fabric. They prevent you from overcutting with the razor.*

Fig. 10-3. *(above, right) Cut a diagonal line to prepare the cloth to be wrapped tightly to the back side.*

Fig. 10-4. *(right) An ATG gun dispenses a line of adhesive that will secure the cloth to the reverse of the mat.*

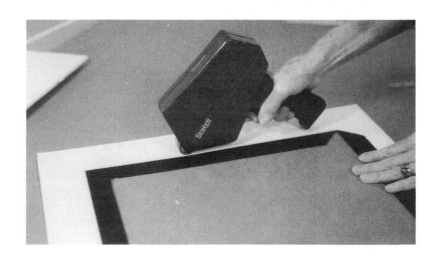

8. Pull the cloth around to the back onto the adhesive (Fig. 10-5). If you prefer not to use glue, you can tape the cloth in place.

9. While you are attaching the cloth, use your razor blade, if needed, to cut the area back a little more toward the corners. Cover the bevel at the corners, so none of the mat peeks through.

10. Repeat and cover the other three sides.

TRIPLE YOUR PLEASURE:
THREE TIERS OF FABRIC-WRAPPED MATS

To reflect the slightly humorous subject matter of the lithograph in Fig. 10-6, we decided to use not one but three layers of fabric-wrapped mats. The glass is between the first and second mat. Figure 10-7 shows the front of the first mat that will be placed next to E. M. Plunkett's artwork, *Salon d'Automne - 1913*. Note that the fabric does not cover the board, as only a small amount of fabric will show in the finished framing job.

First we cut a foam core mat to rabbet dimensions. A narrower window is cut in this foam core. When it is turned over with the bevel facing away from the artwork, the foam core will not be seen. The black fabric mat (featured in Figs. 10-1 through 10-5) is then glued to this foam core. Figure 10-8 shows this black mat, which will be glued to the foam core, being positioned over the first fabric-wrapped mat.

A second piece of foam core for the top mat is also cut to rabbet dimensions, with an even narrower window. Figure 10-9 shows this final mat being placed in position on top of the other two fabric-wrapped mats.

SILK MATS

There are many types of fabric-covered mat boards available, and you should know how to use them if you do not want to cover your own mat board with fabric. Because silk is not the type of fabric one is likely to have in a scrap bag. We used a silk mat board by Bainbridge for this project. This mat has a definite air of formality. It is not too difficult to cut a silk mat board, but there are a few tricks you should know.

1. Cut your outside dimensions.

2. Decide on the width of the mat. In this case, it is 1½ inches.

3. Cut an opening ½ inch larger than the final opening will be. In this case, the window mat is cut as if you wanted a 2-inch mat. Remove the dropout.

4. Practice! Practice! Practice! Use the piece that has dropped out for your first attempt. Score the window mat to cut through the board but not through the silk. Cut from the back, marking your scoring line at 1½ inches.

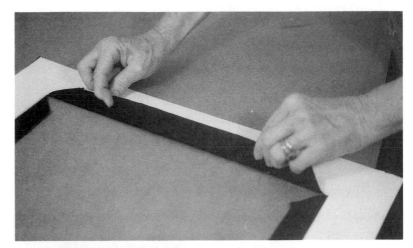

Fig. 10-5. *Pull the cloth taut over the adhesive.*

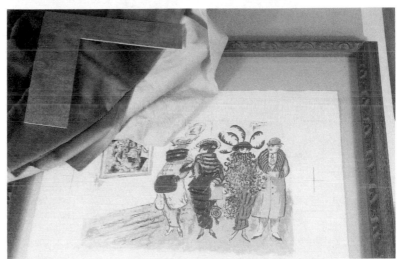

Fig. 10-6. *E. M. Plunkett's* Salon d'Automne-1913, *with suggested fabrics and mats to be used in framing this work.*

Fig. 10-7. *Because only a small portion of the cloth will be seen in the finished job, the fabric does not have to extend the full length of the mat board. This is the first liner mat.*

Fig. 10-8. *Positioning the black middle fabric mat.*

Fig. 10-9. *(left) The fabric extends to the outer edges of the top fabric-wrapped mat because the entire mat is visible in the sight area.*

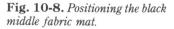

Fig. 10-10. *(bottom left) Remove the cardboard from the back of the silk so the cloth can be wrapped to the back of the mat. Start the process with a razor blade to separate cloth from the board in the scored area.*

Fig. 10-11. *(bottom right) Close-up of fabric-wrapped mat with a dark-colored liner mat with white bevel.*

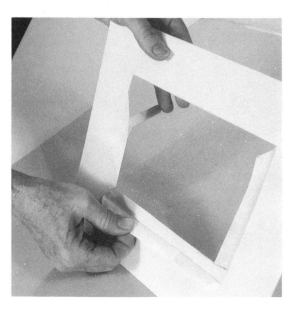

5. Figure 10-10 shows the board being peeled off from the back, leaving the silk, which is quite stiff. Work it a little with your fingers (very clean fingers!) to make it more pliable.

6. Cut diagonally into the corner, as shown in Fig. 10-10. Fold the silk under and around to the back of the mat. Glue it to the back with adhesive or tape. The rest of the procedure is exactly the same as for a regular wrapped mat.

A liner was cut from a grey, acid-free mat board (Fig. 10-11).

11:

POSTERS-
ALWAYS "IN"

In addition to the basic tools and materials listed in Chapter 5, the following items are used to frame or display posters:

Materials	Tools
Uni-Frame (inexpensive hanging device using plastic grippers and cord) • hanging clips • Colormount (bonding tissue)	no new tools

Posters are an easy answer to the question of what can be done to decorate a room, from a college dorm to an executive suite. Their popularity continues to grow, with reproductions from America's finest museums selling almost as many reprints as those blowups of the current television heartthrob.

Prints are easy to display. Almost too easy, in fact. Some will put a poster up with double-faced tape or thumbtacks, and then complain because they wrinkle and bend or tear. If you're really interested in having a poster last longer than the time span of a current fad, it should be properly mounted. Even if you try to frame it without mounting, it will tend to slip or curl or go wavy on you.

You can spray a poster, or use regular glue, and position it on foam core. If it is large and rolled up, this might be a two-person job. Probably the most satisfactory way of dealing with a large poster is to take it to a professional framer and have it dry-mounted. Then you can take it home and handle it in a variety of ways, depending upon its importance and life expectancy.

Figure 11-1 shows a selection of different, inexpensive ways to hang up a poster. The small clips that fold in the center can be pressed into foam core. There are also variations on the plastic holders shown here. Some clip to each side. Some hold the four corners.

HANDLING SMALL POSTERS

Figure 11-2 shows a reprint of an old yachting poster that had been left rolled in a tube and was quite curled up. This was dry-mounted on foam core, and then hung, using one of the folding clips that press

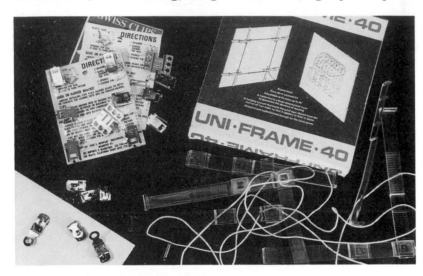

Fig. 11-1. *(above) A selection of poster hanging devices.*

Fig. 11-2. *(left) Yachting poster, before mounting.*

into the back. This works well with lightweight posters. This size poster is easily mounted with spray adhesive or the PMA system (see Chapter 9, Figs. 9-16 to 9-18).

The easiest of all ways to mount something is shown in Fig. 11-3). Take something to use as a mounting board (in this case, a piece of mat board), then add a sheet of mounting paper (here we are using Colormount, a commercial bonding tissue), the certificate or whatever it is you want to mount, and release paper. Instead of release paper, you can use ordinary kraft paper or plain wrapping paper. Then simply iron it (Fig. 11-4), and you have a completed job. You might have encountered this process in grade school or scout camp.

Figure 11-5 is an example of what to do if you have a mounting assignment where someone wants a page from a newspaper mounted.

Fig. 11-3. *Positioning the release paper for ironing.*

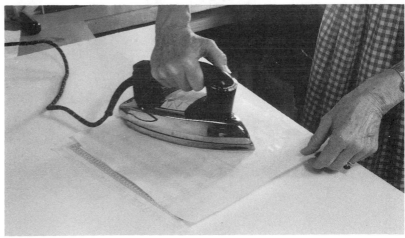

Fig. 11-4. *Mounting using a regular iron.*

Because the ink will bleed through if you use light-colored mounting board, the secret is to mount it on black. A step up from the above would be to use a metal frame, in which you can use either glass or Plexiglas.

HANDLING LARGE POSTERS

Figure 11-6 is a Steichen poster that has special meaning for its owners. It was dry-mounted, a double-rag mat was added, and it was placed in a wood frame. The frame looked and felt very substantial, but once the "package" was put together with glass, the frame bowed, and we could see it pulling away from the package. The solution was to place two mirror hooks on the top and two on the bottom of the frame. Wire was strung in an **X** shape from one to the other, pulling the frame together as tightly as possible (Fig. 11-7). The design of this particular frame was wide enough on the back to accept this kind of hardware.

This type of bowing might happen with long or large metal frames, as well. To brace a metal frame, see Chapter 15 (Figs. 15-5 to 15-7).

You can frame the same Monet poster for four different types of settings. For a child's room, you can use a thin contemporary wood

Fig. 11-5. *Newspaper page is mounted to black mat board so the type will not show through from the reverse side.*

Fig. 11-6. *The Steichen poster.*

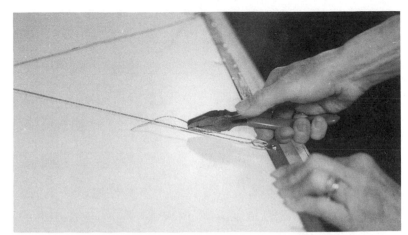

Fig. 11-7. *Tighten the wires to reinforce the frame from bowing.*

Fig. 11-8. *Fasten the strainer to frame with brass screws, two to each side.*

Fig. 11-9. *The Monet poster is mounted to foam core for student's room.*

Fig. 11-10. *The movie memorabilia poster is mounted for permanent protection with mat, under glass, in a builder's molding frame.*

frame, as we did. This frame is too narrow to accept the mirror hooks used on the Steichen poster, however. Instead, we built a strainer. Using the same principle as we did for the construction of a parting strip, we abutted the lengths of wood, which were measured to fit exactly within the frame. You also can use corrugated nails or staples to strengthen these abutted corners.

We then drilled holes through the outside of the frame, into the strainer and used brass screws (Fig. 11-8) to wed the frame to the strainer. Screw eyes were then placed sideways on the inside of the strainer (also Fig. 11-8) and the wire added. This system works well with most frames that are not strong enough to hold the weight of glazing, artwork, backing, and filler board. The Monet that was framed to hang in the executive boardroom used the mirror hooks, as used on the Steichen job, creating the same type of holding leverage. The silver frame for the Monet designed to be hung in a living room did not need extra support. For the student's room (Fig. 11-9), the Monet was treated as inexpensively as we could while still protecting it: it was held in a Uni-Frame (a commercial hanging device shown in Fig. 11-1) with Plexiglas.

For the *Close Encounters with the Stars* poster (Fig. 11-10), a frame was built out of builder's molding with a parting strip added. The poster was mounted and a very narrow mat added to complete the framing.

12:

FRAMING
NEEDLEPOINT

In addition to the basic tools and materials listed in Chapter 5, the following items are used in framing needlepoint:

Materials

polyester batting • lacing thread • nail hole filler • finishes (acrylic spray sealer, spray paint, rub-on paint) • disposable plastic gloves • tacking iron

Tools

a board large enough to block each needlepoint • marking pen • needles • pins • staple gun • tacking iron

Needlepoint looks best when framed simply. Normally we recommend that the frame be cut first, and then the backing boards, glass, and other materials. With needlepoint, you cannot do this. You need to block the needlepoint first and place it on a backing board before you can measure the size of your frame. You normally do not use glass when framing anything made of wool. Wool has a tendency to retain moisture, and when enclosed, this can lead to rot. In most competitions, your needlepoint will not be accepted if it is under glass.

BLOCKING YOUR NEEDLEPOINT

After you have put your last stitch in the needlepoint, your next step to get it ready for framing is to block it. Some make a big deal of this, but it is really very simple. You do not need to buy those special tools, blocking boards, or prepared solutions that are on the market. Here, step by step, is how to take your unblocked needlepoint and block it, mount it, and get it ready for framing. Builder's corner molding is used for the needlepoint on the left in Fig. 12-1.

Fig. 12-1. *Framed needlepoints.*

1. On a board a few inches larger than your needlepoint, attach a sheet of kraft paper. Map out your blocking area on kraft paper. Make sure your corners are square (Fig. 12-2).

2. Locate the centers of each side on the kraft paper and mark them. Fold your needlepoint in half and mark the center of each side with a rustproof pin (Fig. 12-3).

3. Lightly spray or sprinkle water on the needlepoint. Do not soak it because the colors might run. Stretch and pull the needlepoint into shape over the blocking area. Line up your centering pins with the halfway marks on your kraft paper (Fig. 12-4).

4. Block the bottom of the needlepoint along the premarked line on the kraft paper. Note the pin has a staple straddling it. Staple all four centering marks this way. Then add additional staples, starting from the center and working your way out to each corner. Pull and block as you go. Set the needlepoint aside to dry (Fig. 12-5).

5. When dry, remove the staples. Cut a sturdy, durable board to the size of the needlepoint. Cut a polyester filler, also to size, to give fullness to the needlepoint once it is in the frame. If your needlepoint is of value, add a sheet of acid-free board between the polyester and the backing board (Fig. 12-6).

6. Position your needlepoint over the polyester and pin it to the backing board. Put a pin in the approximate center of each of the four sides, then examine the front to be sure you have positioned your design correctly. If satisfactory, pin the piece to hold it in place for lacing. Do not push the pins in very deep because you will be removing them as soon as you have laced the needlepoint across the back.

7. To lace the piece, draw the stitches taut, locking them occasionally as shown in Fig. 12-7. When laced, remove your pins.

8. Make your frame, as instructed in Chapter 2.

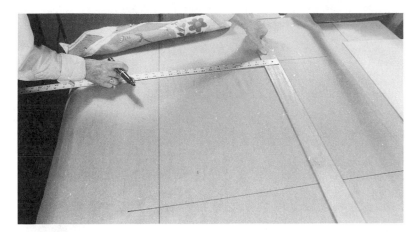

Fig. 12-2. *Map out your blocking area.*

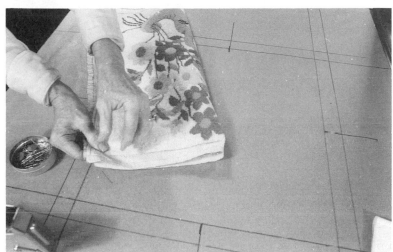

Fig. 12-3. *Locate and mark the center of each side of your needle-point and the kraft paper.*

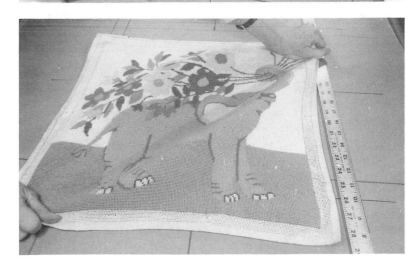

Fig. 12-4. *Pull the needlepoint into shape over the blocking area.*

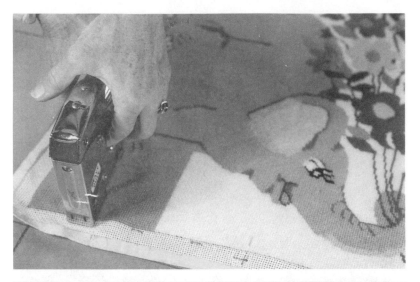

Fig. 12-5. *Block the bottom of the needlepoint by stapling along your premarked line.*

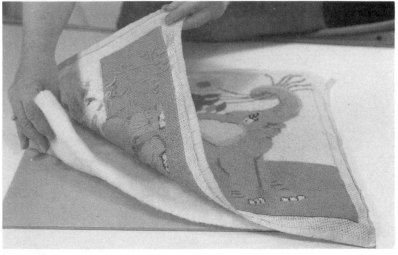

Fig. 12-6. *Cut a sturdy board and polyester filler to the size of the needlepoint. Add an acid-free sheet between them if necessary.*

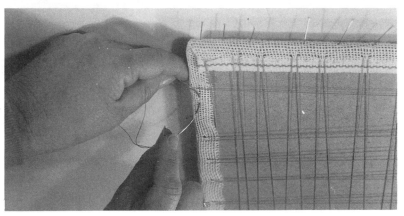

Fig. 12-7. *Pin the needlepoint to the backing board. Lace across the back, drawing the stitches taut and locking them in place.*

126

USING A FOAM-CORE BACKING

The needlepoint in Fig. 12-1 (right) has been blocked and is now ready to be mounted to foam core.

1. Cut the foam core to size (Fig. 12-8).

2. Pin the needlepoint to the foam core. Again, do not push the pins in very deep because you will remove them after stapling (Fig. 12-9).

3. Staple across the back. Start with a staple in the center of each side. Check the front to make sure the needlepoint is still properly aligned. Complete the stapling. Again, work from the center out to each corner (Fig. 12-10).

4. Make a frame of builder's molding and construct a parting strip of ¾-inch wood. As the parting strip will be flush to the outside of the frame, fill the holes with nail hole filler (Fig. 12-11).

5. Clamp the finished parting strip to the frame and nail and glue. Place cinch clamps on the corners and set the parting strip aside to dry. Note the strips of mat board between the clamps and the wood. These prevent the clamps from denting the soft wood (Fig. 12-12).

☞ To eliminate small dents in wood, take a slightly damp cloth or paper towel, hold it against the dent, and apply heat. Here we are using a tacking iron (Fig. 12-13). You can also use the point of a regular iron.

☞ Another optional tool, the ELPA (a brad driver), can be used to close the back of the needlepoint frame. Note the block of wood used to absorb the "kick" from this fitting tool (Fig. 12-14).

Fig. 12-8. *Cut the foam core to size.*

Fig. 12-9. *Pin the needlepoint to the foam core.*

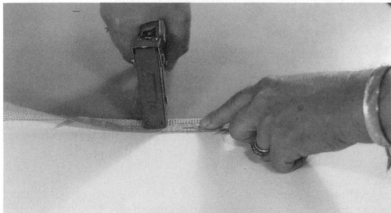

Fig. 12-10. *Staple across the back, working from the center out to each corner.*

Fig. 12-11. *Fill the nail holes of the parting strip.*

Fig. 12-12. *Clamp the parting strip to the frame and nail and glue.*

Fig. 12-13. *Use a tacking iron to eliminate small dents.*

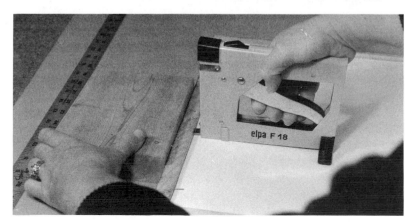

Fig. 12-14. *Use a brad drive to close the back of the frame.*

13:
SHADOW BOXES -WHAT'S IN A FRAME

In addition to the basic tools and materials listed in Chapter 5, the following items are used in this chapter:

Materials

aerosol air spray • awl • DAX box (plastic frame) • decorative button • glazing points • inserts and spacers (wood lathing, mat board, Innerspace, Framespace III) • Mighty Mounts (commercial mounting devices) • PMA material • silk-covered paper • velvet • hardware (turnbuttons, sawtooth hanger)

Tools

X-Acto knife • needle and thread

WHAT'S IN A SHADOW BOX?

What's in a shadow box? Anything you want to display or just protect from marauding children.

A shadow box is an excellent way to display anything that has depth. There are limitless variations on how to construct a shadow box. There are frames within frames or boxes within frames. The variations begin when you decide how much extra decoration you need to display a specific item. Do you want an ornate frame? A velvet lining? Fabric-wrapped liners? It's up to you. Every project offers new, and fascinating challenges.

Restrict your imagination to the bounds presented by the object to be contained. The first consideration is the size of the object you want shadow boxed—how big, how deep, how wide, how heavy. A

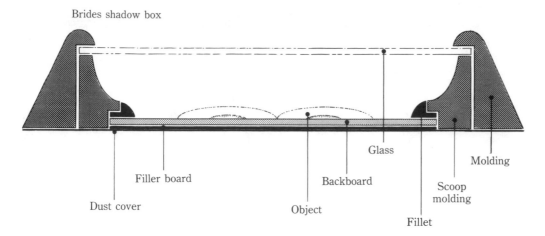

Brides shadow box

Glass

Molding

Filler board

Backboard

Scoop molding

Dust cover

Object

Fillet

collection of tomahawk heads will call for sturdier construction than how to frame Aunt Rose's needlepoint.

Figure 13-1 shows a cutaway diagram of the basic shadow box in Fig. 13-2: the frame within a frame. The inner frame is made using the same techniques used to make another frame, but the molding is selected to give the proper depth for displaying a specific object. They fit together in much the same way as an insert fits between an oil canvas and its frame, with the exception that the glass is included here. Figure 13-3 shows a close-up of the lower left-hand corner. With the various types of builder's molding, you can create a variety of frames.

Each of the examples that follow show easier ways to make the shadow box insert. As you already know the basics of constructing the outer frame, the emphasis is on variations of how to display an object in the frame using inserts, spacers, or other imaginative devices.

Fig. 13-1. *The diagram shows a basic frame within a frame type of shadow box.*

A MEXICAN STANDOUT

Figure 13-4 is an example of a Mexican wall hanging in a shadow box (the long, thin one on the left.) The frame selected is builder's corner molding just deep enough to display the fabric and contain a decorative filler board and a piece of glass.

The basic problems are how to display the fabric and how to hold the glass in place. In this case, let the fabric hang loose, using a decorative button to hold the loop of wool that came with the hanging. Choose colors to accent the bright ones in the fabric. Paint the frame yellow as well as the screen lathing that will be used as a spacer to hold the glass in place. This lathing is made with decorative grooves that show slightly inside the frame.

Normally we suggest that you complete the wood frame; sand, seal, and paint it: and set it aside while you complete the other parts of the package that will go into the frame. In this case, the shadow

Fig. 13-2. *The bride's gown is mounted to old print. The diagram in Fig. 13-1 is of this shadow box.*

Fig. 13-3. *Lower left-hand corner of the bride's shadow box. Note the fillet insert between the two frames.*

box just keeps building. When the outer frame is ready to paint, the spacers/lathes are sprayed yellow at the same time.

Cut the glass to size and clean it. As soon as the frame is dry, place it face down and insert diamond glazing points into the glass (Figs. 13-5 and 13-6) to hold it on what would be the top of the shadow box. (As other elements are added to your shadow box, make sure the glass stays dust free.) The spacers (Fig. 13-7) give the glass added support as well as provide a lip near the back of the frame to hold a filler board and the rest of the framing package.

Fig. 13-4. *Shadow box sample projects.*

As a decorative backboard, attach a bright green mat board to a thin sheet of foam core, which also acts as a filler board. For convenience, mount the mat board and filler board with a Vacuseal press (a vacuum-operated mounting press), though it can be done easily without special equipment. Use regular glue, adhesive spray, or the PMA method (see Chapter 9).

Glue the decorative button in position with a clear silicone. Position the Mexican wall hanging on the green mat board, wrap the wool loop around the button, and insert the package into the back of the frame. Recheck for dust, use a blast from an aerosol can of air spray, then recheck for dust again. Use standard closing brads along with a dust cover to close the back.

SEE DICK AND JANE IN THEIR SHADOW BOX

See the primer. See the primer in the shadow box made of drip cap builder's molding. See the authors make a mistake in measuring. One side of this wood has a slanted edge, leading up to a lip that can be used as a rabbet, with the glass being held in position with glazing points. Because we are accustomed to cutting the backboard and glass the same size, we goofed. The glass is smaller. So, we had to cut it a second time.

The size of the frame was decided, and the wood measured, cut, assembled, sanded, sealed, and finished with a rub-on silver. Figure 13-8 shows the basic Dick and Jane shadow box components: the buffed frame, the primer, two mat boards, a filler board, and four strips of mat board that were cut to serve as decorative spacers on the sides of the shadow box (in addition to the glazing points.)

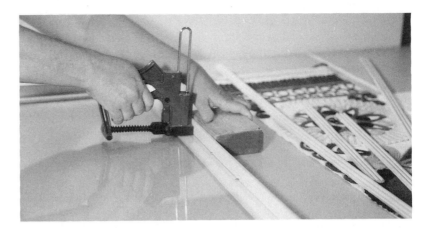

Fig. 13-5. *Insert glaziers points with a point driver. Hold a block of wood behind the frame to absorb the shock. In background: the Mexican wall hanging that will go in the frame and its spacers.*

Fig. 13-6. *The cabinet acts as shock absorber (to demonstrate alternate way). You can crack either the frame or the glass without some form of bracing.*

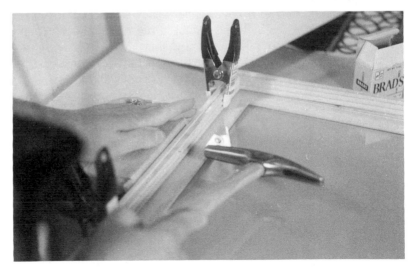

Fig. 13-7. *Once spacers have been glued in position, add nails for additional security. Pressure clamps hold spacers in position until nailing is completed.*

The little see-through items at center right of Fig. 13-8 are Mighty Mounts, versatile shadow box item holders, that will display the primer. These, plus the fact that the back will be removable, permit the owner to turn the pages and display a different spread in the book.

After over fifty years, the colors in the primer are still beautiful. For a backing on which the primer will float, we cut two pieces of mat board: the outside yellow and the inner blue to match the basic colors in the book. The boards were adhered together and then to the filler board.

This unit was designed to be removed easily. Figure 13-9 shows a close-up of these Mighty Mounts. After the primer was positioned on the mat board and filler board, spots were marked where these mounts would be inserted. (If you plan to mount a dish or plate and display it, you could use the longer of these two types of mounts to hold it.) Figure 13-10 shows the back of the frame with the filler board in position so that the turnbuttons show. (*Turnbuttons* are hardware that swivel, mounted on the back of the frame, and make it possible to remove the primer easily.)

☞ If you are mounting anything in a shadow box that will require cleaning or occasional polishing (such as silver spoons), be sure you design the insert box to be removable.

Figure 13-11 shows the back of the frame with the Mighty Mount washers in place and the excess plastic nipped off. You get a little plastic gizmo with these mounts to use as a tool to cinch the mounts to a washer in its final position. Instructions with each package are very easy to follow. Before you insert the mounts, make sure they are positioned properly, then punch a hole with an awl. Before you do any hole punching, position the item (in this case, the primer) while holding the mounts and marking where they should go. Even after you have punched the hole and mounted the item, it can be moved as long as you have not fastened the washer on the back and nipped off the excess plastic. (Try to err on the side that any extra holes you punch will be covered by the object to be displayed. Otherwise, you might have to insert a plastic rose to cover any mistakes seen by the viewer.)

We wiped the glass free of fingerprints and dust and inserted glazing points. In Fig. 13-12 you see where the four siding strips of mat board have been daubed with glue and inserted. They were clamped in position with spring clamps, until dry.

☞ When using mat board or foam core for parting strips or spacers, be sure to leave enough space at each end for them to breathe. Do not butt them tightly, or they will buckle and pop out from the center on the first humid day. If you leave breathing room, they will be okay.

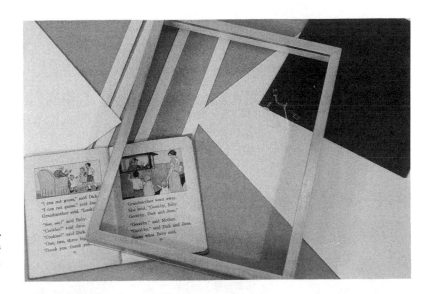

Fig. 13-8. *Basic contents of primer shadow box: frame, two mats, mat board spacers, Mighty Mounts, primer, backing, glass.*

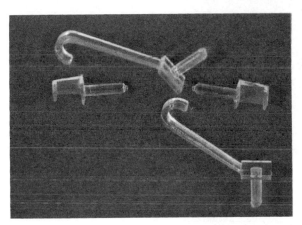

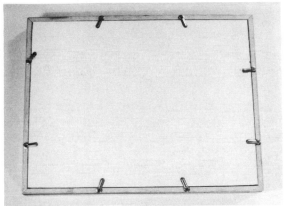

Fig. 13-9. *(above, left) Mighty Mounts are plastic holders for displaying objects in shadow boxes.*

Fig. 13-10. *(above, right) Back of primer shadow box shows turnbuttons that permit the in-and-out feature that make it possible to change the pages displayed.*

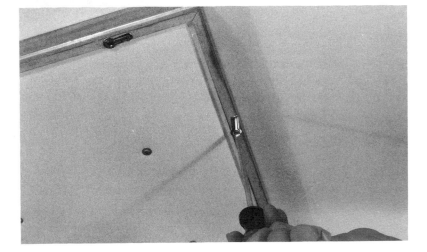

Fig. 13-11. *(right) Mighty Mount washers in place on backing board. Snip off excess plastic.*

The completed primer is shown in Fig. 13-4, lower right. Note—no plastic roses!

FRAMING ELLIE ALABAMA'S TAIL FEATHERS

Years ago, Ellie Alabama, a parrot, shed beautiful bright colored feathers, which were made into a fan. It seemed a shame to leave the fan wrapped in tissue in a trunk, so a shadow box was designed to display it (see Fig. 13-4, upper right). Its bright yellow background emphasizes the brilliance of the feathers. This material (bright yellow mat board) was mounted to 1/8-inch foam core. The back for the shadow box was cut from this, along with four strips to be used as decorative siding. These

Fig. 13-12. *Place mounted primer into the back of shadow box, which is made of drip cap builder's molding.*

Fig. 13-13. *Sew the feathered fan into the foam core backing board.*

138

strips would double as spacers, similar to the ones used in the primer shadow box, holding both the glass and the backing board in position.

Framing molding was selected for the outside frame. Because the rabbet wasn't deep enough to hold the contents of this shadow box, a parting strip was added.

The fan was attached to the backing board, using needle and thread (Fig. 13-13). To hold the feathers away from the board, two small pieces of foam core were placed behind them. These were glued to the backing board, with the feathers resting on them. An additional piece of foam core was cut to the approximate size of the handle, painted black, and glued to the backing board. It was first sewn to the handle and is so inobtrusive that it does not show in the photographs. The end effect gives an illusion that the fan is suspended in the box with space all around the feathers.

The foam core spacers were glued to the sides of the frame after the glass had been secured with glazing points. As with the spacers in the primer box, breathing space was left at each corner so they could expand and contract (Fig. 13-14). Figure 13-14 also shows the fan on its backing board being placed on these spacers.

A BOXED BRACELET

Rather than have a broken clasp repaired on a bracelet, the owner chose to have it displayed in a shadow box. Because the rabbet on

Fig. 13-14. *Position foam core spacers in the framer's molding frame. Because the rabbet is not deep enough, add parting strips to give extra depth to the frame.*

the framer's molding was not quite deep enough to accommodate the contents, a parting strip was added. In this case, the molding and the parting strip were glued together, with nails partially driven through the parting strip into the molding, until the glue was set. This was done so that the nails could be removed before the combined wood was placed in the miter box, and the miters cut. (If your saw ever hits a nail, it could be damaged permanently.)

Figure 13-15 shows the completed shadow box, two dummies, and a sample piece of fabric to demonstrate the ease of making this type of insert box. The foam core on the lower left shows how the box was marked for scoring and cutting. The solid lines will be scored (not cut all the way through) and folded up into sides to become a box. The dotted lines will be cut away, so the corners can be taped to form a perfectly rectangular box. The fabric in the middle is cut slightly oversize and will be glued to the pattern cut from the scored foam core. The box on the right has the corners cut away; the solid lines have been scored, but not cut through, and folded.

One caution in measuring your box. (Practice this once with scrap pieces so that you fully understand. It really is simple.) Figure the size you need for the base of the box, so that it will fit snugly into the rabbet of the frame. Consider that the sides will be the exact width of the foam core you are using. If you are using ⅛-inch foam core and want to have a box that will fit into an area that measures 3 × 6 inches, block off an area that is 3 × 6 inches, but do not make your solid lines yet. Move that line in by ⅛ inch all around, which will give you a solid line that measures 2¾ × 5¾ inches. If your box is 1 inch deep, make the sides ⅞ inch deep to accommodate folding up from the bottom to form the sides. This sounds more complicated than it is. Cut one once, and you will see this is the simplest form of shadow box insert discussed so far.

☞ For a really simple shadow box insert, take a strong cardboard lid from a box that is the size you can use to hold an object you want to display. Then, line this box with decorative paper or fabric and cut a frame to accommodate the size of the box lid, using turnbuckles to hold the insert in position.

The fabric used to display the bracelet is silk mounted to paper. This is a commercial product used to cover mat boards and is similar to some cloth wallpapers. Cut your pattern and spread glue (or spray it on) over the paper side. Press it against your scored and cut pattern made from foam core. Roll it, or press it flat, forcing out all the air. With a razor blade or X-Acto knife, trim away the cloth in the four corners. Bend the corners up and tape them square. Fold the cloth back over the tops of the sides and stick it to the reverse. (The tops of the foam core box look better if the material covers them, in case

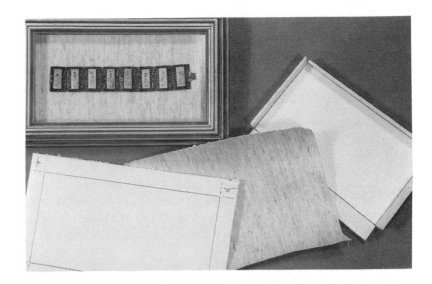

Fig. 13-15. *The completed bracelet shadow box with the foam core dummied to show how to cut and fold insert box.*

Fig. 13-16. *The completed bracelet shadow box.*

Fig. 13-17. *The components for the Dax box shadow box: mats, mat board strips for spacers, doll, foam core, calendar illustration.*

they are slightly wider than the rabbet, and you can see them through the glass.) The bracelet was sewn to the base of the insert box. You can use other devices, but thread seemed to be the most invisible for this project. The finished bracelet shadow box is shown in Fig. 13-16.

A DAX BOX BECOMES A SHADOW BOX

Dax is a commercial name for the plastic picture frame box used for this project. It is another inexpensive and easy way to construct a shadow box. Figure 13-17 shows the components that were used.

   1. Determine what you want to show. We had a small Korean doll. For a background, an illusion was created of a window with a flowering tree in the yard. A mat was cut that would simulate a window behind the doll, off center so that the doll would not clash with the colors in the photograph of the tree.
   2. The picture of a tree in blossom was mounted to foam core backing using PMA (Positionable Mounting Adhesive).
   3. Four strips of mat board were cut to line the sides of the box (Fig. 13-18). These would hide the various levels that would otherwise show through the plastic.
   4. Two mats were cut: one from white mat board and one from foam core that was about ½ inch smaller than the mat board. The foam core mat was reversed, making the bevel invisible, and glued to the first mat. Although you do not see the foam core mat at all, it provides the illusion of distance between the tree and the doll.
   5. Figure 13-19 shows adhesive being applied to the backing board on which the tree picture is mounted. The window mats will be glued to this area.
   6. Figure 13-20 shows a piece of mat board being sewn to the doll's costume. The mat board can then be used to glue the doll to the window mat. Figure 13-21 shows the reverse of this, using a curved needle. Look for an area where you can place a stitch that will not show. The silicone is applied to the mat board (Fig. 13-22). The doll was then glued to the mat.
   7. A tiny hole was drilled into the plastic (Fig. 13-23), on into the foam core. Screws were placed here to hold the package in place.
   8. A sawtooth hanger was glued to the back with silicone because there is no room on this type of frame to place eye screws or wire.
   9. Figure 13-24 shows the completed plastic shadow box.

TWO-FACED SHADOW BOX

The oriental dolls shown in Fig. 13-25 can be viewed from both sides, simply by turning the shadow box around. Three pieces of glass were used for this frame and held in position with Innerspace, a clear plastic strip that is available in various thicknesses. Two of the dolls were sandwiched between the first and second piece of glass. The third

Fig. 13-18. *Insert mat board strips to hide layers in the shadow box. Use white tape to hold corners in position.*

Fig. 13-19. *Apply adhesive with an ATG gun so window mat will adhere to backing board.*

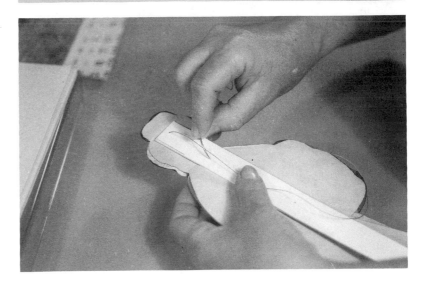

Fig. 13-20. *Sew a strip of mat board to the back of the doll. Mat board will be glued to window mat.*

Fig. 13-21. *Front of doll. Curved needle is easier to use for back and front attaching of this kind.*

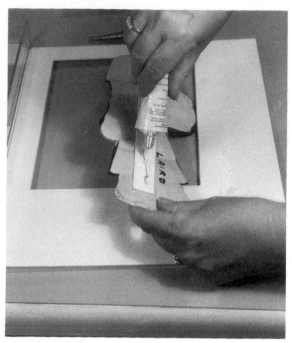

Fig. 13-22. *Silicone glue holds the mat board to the window mat.*

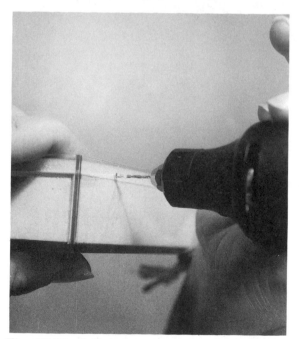

Fig. 13-23. *Drill the holes for the tiny screws that will hold the foam core in position within the plastic frame.*

Fig. 13-24. *Finished oriental doll shadow box.*

144

doll was placed between a third piece of glass and these two. They were glued in position with silicone. The extra piece of glass gives an interesting illusion of depth.

MEDALS OF HONOR

In her lifetime, Hildreth Meière was honored for her contribution in design. Her daughter, author Louise Dunn, plans to frame two of her mother's awards: one from the Architectural League of New York (1928) and the other from the American Institute of Architects (1956). This will offer another approach on how to construct shadow boxes that can be viewed from either side.

As these have sentimental value, a special deep gold framer's molding was ordered "chopped" (precut) to size from a framing store. There is a special framer's molding with an extra built-in rabbet for holding a second piece of glass on the reverse side, but this is not that type, as we want to show you how to use special spacers for this project.

To display the medals, a dark blue velvet was chosen as a good contrast to the gold in the medals and the frame. The A.I.A. medal has a blue ribbon attached to it that also looks good against this velvet.

The medals were framed two different ways, although the end results look the same. Both used two pieces of foam core cut to the size of the frame. In both cases velvet was wrapped around the foam core after an area had been hollowed out from the center to hold the medal.

Figure 13-26 shows the materials used for one of the boxes.

1. The first step is to cut two pieces of foam core the size of the frame, after the frame had been assembled. Cut the hole from the center of each piece, approximately ⅛ inch smaller than the medal. The hole must be smaller or the medal will fall through. The foam core has enough "give" to it to hold and display the medal.

2. Cut a piece of velvet that will wrap around both pieces of foam core when they are sandwiched together. Spray the back of the velvet with adhesive. Figure 13-27 shows the two pieces of foam core, on the velvet, not quite butted together. (Once you have the velvet glued to them, you want to be able to close them, with the velvet fitting tight). Work the velvet through the two holes by cutting the velvet with a razor or X-Acto knife and carefully pulling it over the openings. The idea is to cover all the white of the foam core with velvet to get

Fig. 13-26. *Components for medal shadow box: frame, velvet, spray adhesive, foam core, Framespace spacers, glass, tools, and the medal.*

Fig. 13-27. *After spraying the velvet with adhesive, cut and form it around the opening in the foam core that will display the medal.*

a smooth surface. Do this by slashing off small pieces with your blade as you work the velvet into the hole.

3. With your blade, cut away excess material as you butt the pieces of velvet together. (Because they have the adhesive on the back, these small pieces are easy to position.) You'll get the knack. Use small cuts, butting each one against the one next to it to form a solid blue tunnel through the foam core.

Fig. 13-28. *Cover the clear plastic Framespace with a strip of velvet so only velvet will be seen as a background.*

Fig. 13-29. *Fabric-wrapped Framespace with the final corner being joined. The glass is held in the grooves of the plastic spacer.*

Fig. 13-30. *The finished spacer. The corners are not tightly matched as they need space to expand and contract in the frame. Cut the fabric slightly larger to cover these gaps, which will not show from the front (or back) of the frame.*

4. With the hole edges covered, close the two pieces of foam core as you would shut a book. This is after you have placed adhesive (spray, glue, ATG gun) on the two pieces of foam core. Force the medal into position, and as long as you have kept the hole smaller than the medal, it will fit perfectly. The foam core will give enough to hold the medal.

Fig. 13-31. *Insert the spacer from the back of the frame. Screw the second piece of glazing (Plexiglas) to the back of the frame.*

Fig. 13-32. *Viewed from the back, H. Meière's 1956 medal— the first ever awarded a woman from the A.I.A.*

Fig. 13-33. *Hildreth Meière and her two medals. In 1928 she received the Architectural League of New York's gold medal for painting. In 1956, the A.I.A. awarded her their gold medal for excellence in mural painting and mosaics.*

For the second medal, the two pieces of foam core were glued together first, and then the velvet was worked into the center of the two pieces. This proved to be a little more difficult to do and still maintain a perfect look. There was a tendency for the velvet to have small jagged edges peeking through on the side that was done last.

For both frames, mount glass into a commercial product called Framespace III, a clear plastic spacer that holds glass in position with a frame. The III indicates it is thicker (or wider) than Framespace I or II. Cover the face of these spacers with the velvet cloth (Fig. 13-28). Spray the strips of velvet with adhesive. Each frame has one set of four pieces of Framespace III to hold the glass in the frame. Figure 13-29 shows the fourth piece being pressed onto the glass. With these spacers, as with the mat board spacers, you must be careful to leave breathing space in each corner, or they will pop out. There will be some expansion and contraction with changes in humidity. To be sure this entire area is covered, cut the velvet slightly longer than the plastic strips so this small gap in each corner is not visible. Figure 13-30 shows the piece of glass, with the plastic and velvet in place, before it was put into one of the frames (Fig. 13-31). Figure 13-32 shows the back view of one of the medals. Figure 13-33 shows a bust of Hildreth Meiere and her two framed medals.

14:
HERE, THERE, AND EVERYWHERE

In addition to the basic tools and materials listed in Chapter 5, the following items are used in the projects in this chapter:

Materials

burlap • finishes (Treasure Gold) • black core mat board • silk mat • imitation silk mat • molding (framer's and builder's, wood fillets, metal frame) • spacers (Innerspace) • turpentine • removable Scotch tape • wood substitute (Masonite)

Tools

C&H Cutter (a professional mat cutter)

After you have framed various types of artwork and objects, you will find that each new project offers a different, individual challenge. The projects here are exercises in just that—using different materials imaginatively. We'll show you when to add something to give a print or photo individuality; how to show both sides of an item; what to add to two or more related jobs to give them a more definite relationship in the framing, yet approaching each job as an individual project. The first two projects demonstrated here are in this last category.

FRAMING TWO RELATED ITEMS

Everyone has a certificate or print that has been kicking around the attic or the bottom of your closet waiting to be framed "someday." With your framing knowledge, that someday is now.

The first of these two attic items is a wedding certificate (see Fig. 14-4). Because it is small, and somewhat ornate, we will use a narrow gold frame that reflects the gold design in the certificate. Figure 14-1 shows the ½-inch framer's molding being assembled in the miter vise. (There are other photographs and text showing this frame being cut in Chapter 2, Figs. 2-21 and 2-22). The gold finish (Treasure Gold) is first thinned with turpentine (Fig. 14-2) to give it a slightly duller finish than it would have if applied full strength. After applying the thinned finish, rub it to a shine.

The mat used on this certificate is a *Silkie* (looks like silk, but isn't) because the silk look complements the color and formality of the certificate. The gold liner complements both the certificate and the frame. Brads are inserted to hold the assembled package in place before the dust cover is glued on to the back (Fig. 14-3).

A companion piece for the certificate is a framed photograph of the couple walking down the aisle. In Chapter 1, Fig. 1-8 shows most of the elements used for this project: the photograph, a double mat

Fig. 14-1. *Glue the final corner of the frame.*

Fig. 14-2. *Thin the finish with turpentine. Be sure to check the type of thinner to use for the specific finish you are applying.*

152

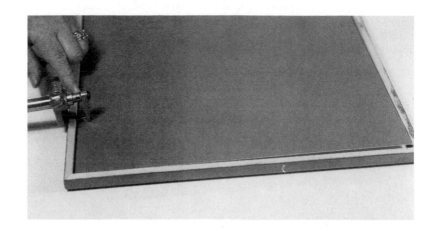

Fig. 14-3. *Use a fit tool to insert brads on back of frame.*

Fig. 14-4. *The two completed frames. Mats, frames, and gold finish are the same on both.*

153

made from the same mat boards as used for the certificate, the backing board, and the glued and nailed frame being held in corner clamps. Both completed projects are shown in Fig. 14-4.

ANOTHER FORMAL WEDDING PORTRAIT

To enhance the matting of this formal portrait, a thin strip of gold wood, called a *fillet*, will be used between the photograph and a silk mat. Figure 14-5 shows the photograph, already mounted on the backing

Fig. 14-5. *Thin gold wooden fillets to be used as liner between picture and silk mat.*

Fig. 14-6. *Close-up of mitered fillets next to the silk mat.*

Fig. 14-7. *A touch of class—the completed frame.*

board, with the silk mat and the pieces of gold wood fillet before they were assembled and glued. If you plan to use fillets, ask your supplier how to cut them or have them cut to size. You can probably use a miter box and saw, or a hacksaw, but double-check this. There also is a pocket miter maker designed specifically for cutting flat molding or wood fillets. The mitered fillet is positioned next to a silk mat (Fig. 14-6). The finished frame is shown in Fig. 14-7. The frame was "chopped" (precut) to order at a framing store and then assembled. In some cases, this might be the only way to get a specific frame design when you are not qualified to buy it in quantity.

SEEING BOTH SIDES OF THE PICTURE

There comes a time when your kid brings something home from school, and you really do want to keep it. What's more, because there's something on both sides, you want to be able to look at both sides. Here's how to handle that situation.

The work shown here was brought home by Andrew Schultz, age five, and proudly presented to his mother. It had a thin paper mat on it. A heavier mat was needed to keep the work away from the glass. The frame, glass, and other elements in this two-sided frame are shown in Fig. 14-8. The backing mat was cut so that the poem, glued on

Fig. 14-8. *Ingredients for two-sided frame: metal frame, two pieces of glass, artwork, double mat, and the backing board/window mat.*

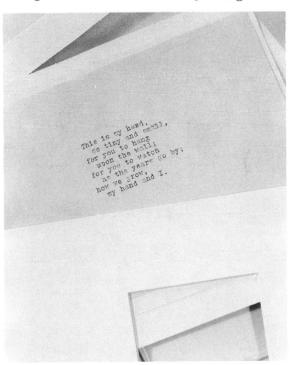

Fig. 14-9. *Cut a window mat in the backing board so the poem on the back of the art can be read.*

155

Fig. 14-10. *The assembled package ready to be inserted into frame. Remember to brace the frame against a solid object when inserting the package.*

Fig. 14-11. *Back view of finished frame.*

Fig. 14-12. *Authors Dunn and Laird in framed mirror.*

the back of the drawing, could be read (Fig. 14-9). These two mats, plus the artwork, were sandwiched between two pieces of glass. The second piece of glass not only allows the poem to be read, it eliminates the need for a filler board (Fig. 14-10). Figure 14-11 shows the completed back view. With this method of framing, "Mom" will always be able to take the frame off the wall and be reminded of this youthful message.

MIRROR, MIRROR ON THE WALL—HORIZONTALLY OR VERTICALLY

No, not Snow White. Those two are your authors in Fig. 14-12. The frame the mirror is in was purchased in a thrift shop for about one-tenth the cost of the mirror glass, but it does make a perfect mirror frame. Figure 14-13 shows how the mirror hooks are placed on two different sides of the back so it can hang vertically or horizontally.

Fig. 14-13. *Mirror hangers. Two sets are used on this mirror to hang them vertically or horizontally.*

Fig. 14-14. *Mat cut from mat board with black core.*

157

FRAMING A CERTIFICATE

If you are framing a certificate, a very effective professional touch can be added by using a special type of mat board. It has a black core. When you cut the bevel, you get the dramatic effect shown in Fig. 14-14. In the framing business, this decorative bevel is called a V groove and was cut by author Dunn using her professional mat cutter (a C & H). Although the V groove takes a professional touch, this type of mat can add an interesting element to your work, especially with certificates or photographs. You cut it as you would a regular mat, but the black core makes the difference, adding that little extra touch of drama.

MEXICAN BARK PAINTINGS

When traveling south of the border, many come back with bark paintings, planning to frame them. Instead, they join a growing pile of "things to frame . . . eventually." This type of souvenir is relatively easy to frame and looks quite distinctive.

Figure 14-15 shows a detail of two Mexican bark paintings. To frame the one on the left, burlap was mounted to Masonite (hardboard made from pressed wood fibers), then the bark painting was mounted to the burlap. White glue was used both times.

The smaller one on the right was framed to give a more sophisticated look. It is floated on a mat board under glass. To prevent the artwork from touching the glass, we used Innerspace (acid-free plastic strips that provide space between art and glazing). Innerspace (Fig. 14-16) comes with a pressure-sensitive backing and adheres directly to the rabbet of the frame.

Fig. 14-15. *Inexpensive bark paintings add a bright touch to rustic decor.*

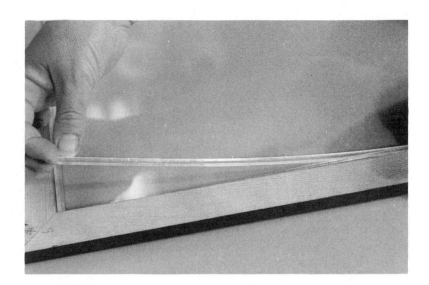

Fig. 14-16. *Innerspace—another device to keep art from touching glass.*

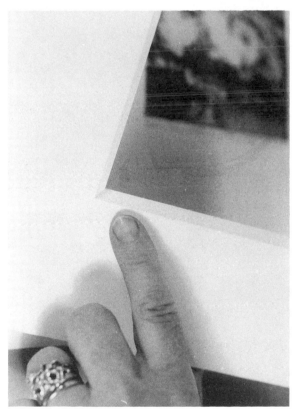

Fig. 14-17. *The bevel in the foam core. This will be reversed, and therefore hidden, to give an added impression of depth for this job.*

Fig. 14-18. *The 1967 etching,* Here, There, and Everywhere, *by artist Marjorie Morrow.*

DEPTH WISH

This is a relatively small etching. To give it added dimension, a fairly large mat was used. As this is a numbered etching and signed by the artist, the mat was cut from 100 percent rag board.

A second mat was cut from 3/16-inch, acid-free foam core (Fig. 14-17), about ½ inch smaller than the first mat. The foam core mat was then turned over, so that the bevel was on the back side, and positioned on the artwork. As you place the larger mat (the first one) on top of the foam core mat, you get an illusion of depth. This use of a reverse bevel foam core mat gives the framing a bit of a shadow box feeling, plus added interest for the print because of the way it is displayed. The finished framing project, photographed on a living room wall, is shown in Fig. 14-18.

15:
PICTURES
IN AN
EXHIBITION

In addition to the basic tools and materials used in making frames and mats, the following items are used:

Materials	**Tools**
810 Scotch Tape (regular magic transparent tape) • corner protectors • shipping and strapping tape	no new tools

Sooner or later, if you haven't done so already, you will be framing your work or that of others for competitions or exhibits. Your first such contact is usually with local art association contests or outdoor shows. The frames on the outdoor display rack in Fig. 15-1 were made according to instructions in Chapters 2 and 5. These are easy to make, and many judges insist on a simple wood or metal frame with a single white mat. The prize-winning framed photograph shown in Fig. 15-2 was also framed using tools and materials discussed in this book. The wood is builder's molding, back band, and was cut using the plastic Stanley Mitre Box illustrated in Fig. 1-3. The joined frame is shown Fig. 1-6.

With the information you have here, you will have no trouble framing or matting your art or photographs. There are a few more things you should know about exhibiting them, however, once you are ready.

If it is your entry, or if you are in any way responsible for someone's entry, be sure you read the instructions for the show very carefully. Follow them to the letter.

SHIPPING ARTWORK

If your artwork is accepted to be shown in an area where it is not convenient for you to deliver it in person, how do you get it there?

Fig. 15-1. *Local art fairs offer excellent opportunities to use your framing skills.*

Fig. 15-2. *The frame on this award winning photograph is the one being cut in Chapter 1, Fig. 1-3. The photographer and frame cutter is Dana Laird.*

Fig. 15-3. *Fred Rawlinson with his award winning watercolor,* Canyon Series #1.

162

For a fee, you can hire a shipping firm specializing in artwork. They will crate, transport, deliver, unpack. After the show, they will reverse the process and return your art work to you. If it is the only way to get your work to that show, you might have to pay that fee.

You might sell an item that the buyer wants shipped to his or her home. It is helpful to know that UPS (United Parcel Service) will come to your home and pick up and deliver on any of their regular routes. Federal Express and other similar firms offer delivery within 24 or 48 hours. Be careful of weight and measurement requirements. There are specific limitations. Packages that are too big or too heavy can sometimes be sent via an interstate bus line (Greyhound, Trailways, etc.). It means a trip to the bus station on both ends, but the package will arrive, and you will be able to exhibit. The painting shown in Fig. 15-3 (Fred Rawlinson's award winning watercolor, *Canyon Series #1*) was shipped to Connecticut via Greyhound and returned to Memphis via UPS for another exhibit.

TAPING THE FRAME

Rawlinson's painting is large (30 × 40 inches) and was framed with Plexiglas, as it was known that it would be shipped when the framing requirements were decided. The frame was reinforced at the same time. Handlers often pick up metal frames by the frame itself instead of the wires. This can cause the frame to bow, and the artwork sometimes will not go back into the proper channel. At the same time, dirt and other matter can get between the Plexiglas and the matted artwork.

To avoid the problem of foreign matter, the entire assembly (glass, mats, artwork, backing board, and filler) was taped around the edges with 810 Scotch Tape (regular magic transparent tape) before the package was inserted into the frame (Fig. 15-4). This idea of taping the entire assemblage is good for any frame where there is easy entry for foreign matter, such as a wood frame finished with a gold or silver that has a tendency to flake and emit metallic dust at the time you are closing the frame.

BRACING THE FRAME

To avoid the problem of the bowing frame, Rawlinson's metal frame was reinforced with extra wire across the back. For this type of bracing, note the hanger in Fig. 15-5. It is standard hardware with many metal frames, but not all. Two of these hangers are placed in the channel in the top portion of the frame, with the eye of each hanger facing down, and two are placed on the bottom of the frame, facing up. The wire is then threaded through the eyes of these hangers, creating an X (Fig. 15-6). These wires are then secured as tightly as you can, manually. After that, take a screwdriver (Fig. 15-7) and tap each hanger toward

Fig. 15-4. *An effective way to keep insects and other foreign matter out of a frame: put tape all around the edge of the package before inserting it into the frame.*

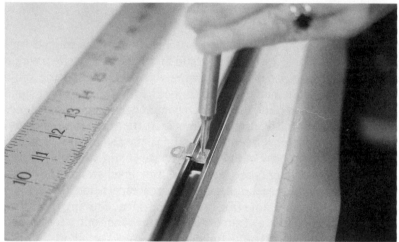

Fig. 15-5. *The first step in reinforcing the frame is to place the screw into the hanger.*

Fig. 15-6. *Attach the second wire to brace the metal frame. This job is made easier when the work is being forced against a solid object or wall.*

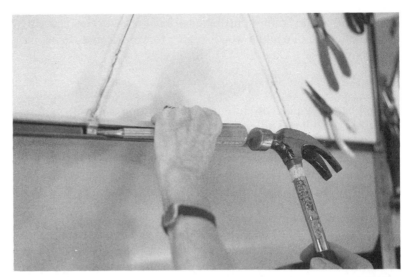

Fig. 15-7. *Make the wire taut by tapping the screw toward the outer edge of the frame.*

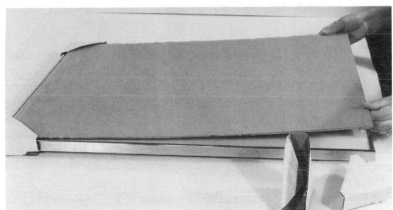

Fig. 15-8. *Protective corners hold cardboard in place for shipping. These are also used to protect frames while being stored or transported.*

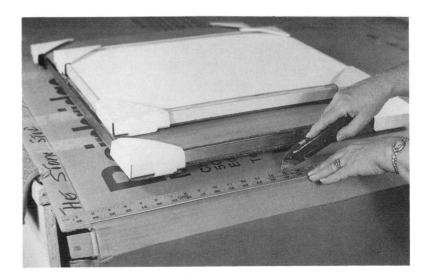

Fig. 15-9. *Score the cardboard using utility knife and straightedge to form a shipping box.*

the outside of the frame, putting additional pressure on the wires to draw them taut. (To add a wood strainer to wood frames to keep them from bowing, see Chapter 11, Fig. 11-8.)

BOXING DAY

An important aspect of shipping art is getting it ready, before the carrier takes over. The easiest way is to take an existing cardboard box and cut it down to size. Before placing the painting in the box, cut two pieces of cardboard slightly smaller than the frames you want to protect. Place one in front, and one in back of the painting, and hold them in place with protective cardboard corners (Fig. 15-8).

☞ *Corner protectors* are very useful if you are continually moving paintings from place to place. Artwork can be stacked more easily using these cardboard corners. They come in various sizes, with some adjustable to fit wide and deep frames. Figure 15-8 shows these corners in use.

In shipping, if you do not have these corner pieces, wad newspapers or cut extra cardboard to protect the artwork. If you are dealing with Plexiglas and metal frames, these packing suggestions should be more than adequate. If you are shipping more delicate work, follow these directions but take them a step or two further. Use bubble wrap around both cardboard padding and the frames. In some cases, pack them as suggested and fill the shipping box with styrofoam or shipping "popcorn." (Some call them plastic "peanuts"—that white plastic stuff that spills all over when you open packages marked *fragile*.)

To cut down existing cardboard, use a utility knife held against a straightedge to score the line you want to bend into a new wall for your box (Fig. 15-9). With the new strapping and shipping tapes, the work of preparing a shipping box is a breeze. Do not forget to insert an extra shipping label inside the box, as well as placing one on the outside.

16:

REFRAMING-
RESCUING OLD
PRINTS & PHOTOS

In addition to the basic tools and materials for making frames and mats, the following items are used:

Materials	**Tools**
regular and rag mats	a household iron

- Gesso • acrylic colors
- Woolite • nonrusting pins

In your eagerness to mat and frame new prints and photos, don't neglect old treasures that have been around so long you don't really notice they are gradually disintegrating. This is not to suggest that you should undertake to repair valuable art treasures that should be sent to a professional conservator. The information in this chapter is designed to help you put a halt to acid or moisture damage by realizing that it is happening. You can then put your grandmother's graduation picture in a new frame, with proper matting and backing.

A good example of a rescue mission you might attempt is the wedding group picture in Fig. 16-1. This photograph was brought in for reframing in its original frame. The picture was right up against the glass, which probably accounts for the water damage on the left. Space between the glass and artwork is necessary to allow trapped humidity to evaporate. There was also acid damage from the wooden backing.

As mentioned in Chapter 6 on Conservation, it is not the fault of the individual framer. At the turn of the century, no one realized that glass would trap moisture and stain the artwork or that wood for a filler or backing could cause acid damage. In reframing this 1892 wedding photo, conservation methods were used. As we do not have the professional expertise of a conservator, the photo was left on its original board. We did not know what adhesive was used to mount

Fig. 16-1. *The wedding of Katherine Robeson Bowen to Frank Marcelus Bailey, near Philadelphia, 1892. (Photograph courtesy of Jere Rowland.)*

it, and felt it would be more dangerous to try to remove it than to leave it alone. A double rag mat was used to keep the picture from touching the glass, and a new rag filler board was inserted.

AN 1890 ETCHING: STRATFORD POINT

A similar problem was encountered with the etching shown in Fig. 16-2. This etching had been signed by the artist who had then added a remarque to the mat in 1890. (A *remarque* is an embellishment added by the artist to a print or etching, generally done in pencil or pen and ink on the mat, along with the artist's signature.) Whoever framed this etching cut it down to fit the frame, which should never be done. The artwork was also butted against the rabbet of the frame, which permitted easy access for the acid in the wood to migrate onto the print. A third deadly sin was committed by using wood as a backing, and not just wood, but wood with a knothole in it. When the back was removed (Fig. 16-3), the knot had burned through to the back of the etching and was beginning to show from the front (Fig. 16-4). You can also see the acid burn that migrated from the bevel in Fig. 16-4.

To get the artwork away from the frame, a slightly larger mat was used. This permitted the etching to be properly hinged to the backing board with conservation hinging. A double rag mat was also used.

☞ In restoring artwork, check the measurements of the art carefully. The left border of this etching was almost ½-inch wider than the right, and the lower margin was uneven. These discrepancies were then taken into consideration in planning the measurements of the window mats.

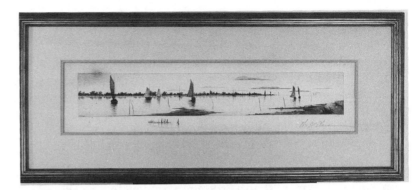

Fig. 16-2. *Signed etching in new frame with conservation mats. Burn on upper left is from the knothole in the original wood backing.*

Fig. 16-3. *(right) The original wood backing and back side of etching.*

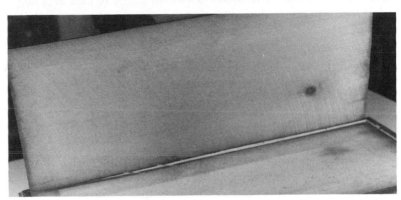

Fig. 16-4. *(bottom left) Close-up of left side of etching that shows the knothole stain plus the migration of acid from the bevel.*

Fig. 16-5. *(bottom right) Turn of the century etching shows an acid burn from the bevel of the partially removed window mat.*

You can also see acid burn clearly in the etching of the old tree in Fig. 16-5. This is another etching of the same period that we rematted and backed with conservation material.

Using the knowledge we have today, we have done what we believe is right. If these etchings had been more valuable, we would have taken other precautions. The price for such steps was greater than the owners felt the etchings were worth, however. We truly hope that 30 years from now, some framer doesn't open up our job and react the way we did in discovering the efforts that were made in the 1890s.

JUST LIKE THE COBBLER'S CHILDREN

As a framer, it is more than a little embarrassing to look around your own home and suddenly realize that there is something on a wall that is literally falling apart. The rubbing (that one crumbling away in Fig. 16-6) had been purchased in Guatemala in 1961. It had survived a variety of climates, but eventually gave up, and the finish on the frame started falling off in chunks.

Figure 16-7 shows the back of the frame. The original framing job was about as primitive as the subject matter it held. The rubbing had been done on good sheeting material but held in position with masking tape.

The first step in restoring the frame was to get the rest of the finish off, which obviously was not too difficult. The wood itself was very sturdy and hard, and it sanded down almost effortlessly. Figure 16-8 shows the reworked frame receiving a first coat of smooth gesso. We texturized the second coat (Fig. 16-9) using some of the same tools mentioned in Chapter 4 (Fig. 4-10). Acrylic color was then mixed and brushed on. Liquid Leaf White Fire (a commercial gold finish) was brushed over the raised texturizing to give a brand new look to the old frame.

Figure 16-10 shows the rubbing after it had been washed in Woolite (cold water soap) and ironed carefully, as we were not certain of the contents of the material used to create the rubbing. It is being pinned to an acid-free foam core board in Fig. 16-11 using nonrusting pins. The revitalized frame and rubbing looked terrific individually but were no longer meant for each other together. After trying various frames in combination with both fabric-wrapped and colored mats, a simple framer's molding was selected, with no matting. This is artwork without dimension and looks best in a relatively flat frame (Fig. 16-12).

The newly revitalized frame was used on a Guatemalan oil, painted in that country's old capital, Antiqua. With its gentle slope inward, the frame highly emphasizes the dimensional qualities of the composition of this painting (Fig. 16-13).

SALVAGING A BEACHED BOAT

A framed silkscreen (Fig. 16-14) was an assignment tossed to us to see if we could do something interesting with the various elements.

Fig. 16-6. *Guatemalan rubbing shows the frame starting to peel.*

Fig. 16-7. *Back side of frame with original framing materials in position.*

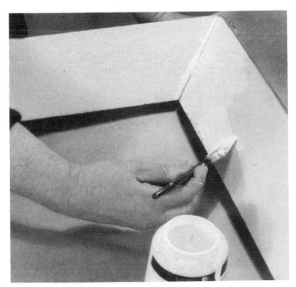

Fig. 16-8. *First apply thin coat of gesso.*

Fig. 16-9. *Apply Liquid Leaf (gold finish) over the texturized gesso.*

Fig. 16-10. *(top right) Newly washed rubbing being placed on a new backing board.*

Fig. 16-11. *(middle right) Rustproof pins hold the rubbing in place on the backing board.*

Fig. 16-12. *(bottom left) The completed project. Washed and ironed, the rubbing is in its new frame.*

Fig. 16-13. *(bottom right) Old frame now houses painting with dimensional composition that gives the illusion of added depth.*

Fig. 16-14. Beached Boat *in its original frame.*

Fig. 16-15. *Gesso that has had acrylic tint added to it is applied to the old frame over a base coat of white.*

Fig. 16-16. *The salvaged* Beached Boat.

The frame was coming apart, and the print needed more dramatic handling. The first step was to take the frame apart and sand it down. Because of its depth, two clamps were used in rejoining it (this is illustrated in Chapter 1, Fig. 1-10). A thin coat of white gesso was painted on the frame, followed by a second coat that had acrylic color added (Fig. 16-15), which complemented the double mat that was used with the print. The salvaged *Beached Boat* (Fig. 16-16) now hangs in a prominent spot in the den.

APPENDIX: TOOLS, MATERIALS, & SUPPLY SOURCES

With few exceptions, the tools and materials used in this book were obtained from local stores in the lower Connecticut area. You should be able to get them from the same types of stores. The builder's molding came from local lumberyards. The unfinished framer's molding came from large hardware stores, craft shops, professional framing suppliers, and the large home-improvement chain stores. The art supplies came from (oddly enough) art supply stores.

We have listed the tools used. If an item is a specialty product, we list the address where you can either obtain the item or find out where you can buy it in your area.

Some of the firms that have mail order departments are also listed as well as large stores that have outlets in various parts of the country. If there is an 800 number, call it or check your yellow pages; perhaps there is an outlet near you.

TOOLS AND MATERIALS

Adhesives
    ATG Dispenser (adhesive transfer gun)
    ATG Tape (refills for the ATG gun)
    Scotch Brand Magic Plus tape
    Scotch Brand 811 tape (transparent removable tape)
    Silicone
    Sobo (white glue)
    Elmer's (white glue)
    Wellbond (wood glue)
    Rice starch
    Wheat starch
Frames—Framing—Finishes
    Denglas (crystal clear antireflective), Denton Vacuum Inc.

Framespace (available from Frametek, 5120-5 Franklin Blvd., Eugene,
Oregon 97403, 800-227-9933)
Innerspace (available from Buckwalter, 43 E. Lancaster Ave., Paoli,
PA 19301, 800-EASYFIT)
Mighty Mounts (available from R & D Framing Co., 529 Deines
Ct., Ft. Collins, Colorado 80525)
Mounting Corners (for holding photos or artwork in place)
Butcher Wax (paste wax)
Tre Wax (paste wax)
Tung oil (wood finish)
Point driver (for holding glazing in place)
Masonite
Metal section frames
Wood section frames
Stretchers (for oil paintings)
Uni-Frame (inexpensive way to hang unframed posters or prints
using plastic grippers and cord)
Dax (plastic framing box)
Foam Core
Glass Cutters
Hinges
Filmoplast
Insta-Hinge
Linen
Japanese paper
Kraft paper If you have trouble buying kraft paper in small quantities,
any heavy-duty paper will work well as a dust cover.
Mat Board
Regular
100% Rag
Acid-free
Mat Cutters
Paints & Thinners
Aerosol-dispensed spray paint
Liquid Leaf
Rub 'n Buff
Treasure Gold
Turpentine (Check instructions on specific paint or finish to determine
which thinner to use).
Miscellaneous Tools
Automatic brad nailers
Break starting pliers for glass cutting
Metal square
Pro-Trim knife (for trimming dust covers)
Tacking iron
Corner clamps

Spring clamps
Miter box
Miter vise
Nail set
Utility knife
Marking gauge
Saw
X-Acto knife
Razor blade

OTHER SPECIAL SOURCES

Stanley Tools, 195 Lake St., New Britain, CT 06050 (manufacturer of complete line of hardware and tools)

Jerry's Artarama, P.O. Box 1105, New Hyde Park, NY 11040; 800-221-2323 (Distributor of a wide variety of framing tools and materials)

American Frame Corp., 1340 Tomahawk Dr., Maumee, OH 43567; 800-537-0944 (metal and wood section frames)

Light Impressions, 439 Monroe Ave., P.O. Box 940, Rochester, NY 14603; 800-828-6216 (Conservation supplies for photography and works of art on paper)

ASW (Art Supply Warehouse), 360 Main Ave. (Rt. 7), Norwalk, CT 06851; 800-243-5038 (general art supplies)

Contemporary Frame Co., Scott Swamp Rd., Rte 6-Dept R, P.O. Box 514, Unionville, CT 06085; 800-243-0386 (metal section frames)

Stu-Art Supplies, 2045 Grand Ave., Baldwin, NY 11510 (general art supplies, frames, precut mats)

Dick Blick Co., Dept AA, P.O. Box 1276, Galesburg, IL 61401 (general art supplies; will ship mat board; catalog $2)

Graphik Dimensions, Ltd., Dept AA, 41-23 Haight, Flushing, NY 11355; 800-221-0262 (frames—metal and wood, general art supplies, and framing tools and supplies)

Glossary

archival—With reference to framing, the relative permanence of a material and its ability to remain stable over time.

assemblage (package)—The putting together of all parts, from glass to backing, prior to inserting into a frame.

ATG gun (Adhesive Transfer Gun)—Commercial adhesive dispenser.

ATG tape—Pressure-sensitive adhesive used in ATG gun.

awl—Pointed tool, resembling an ice pick, used for starting holes for inserting screw eyes or brads.

backboard (substrate)—Support for artwork; the board artwork is hinged to, with filler board behind it in a frame.

backsaw—cutting tool used in miter box; has a stiffened top edge and fine teeth.

bevel—Slanted angle; the cut made for a mat opening; not a right angle.

blocking—System of stretching and shaping fabric (needlepoint, cloth paintings) into a rectangular or framable shape.

brad—Thin nail with very small head.

builder's molding—Wood originally designed for house trim; used in framing with the addition of a parting strip rabbet.

bumper—Corner protrusion added to lower back corners of a frame to keep the frame from touching the wall and to allow ventilation.

cockling—Wrinkling or puckering in paper generally caused by moisture.

conservation—Use of state-of-the-art methods to preserve works of art; framing to museum standards.

conservation framing—The use of museum standards employing acid-free materials such as museum board, Japanese hinges, museum board substrate, rice or wheat paste, methyl cellulose, and acid-free filler board.

corner clamp—Device used to hold two sides of a frame while their 45-degree mitered corners are glued and nailed.

countersink—To push a nail beneath the surface of the wood; done with a nail set.

dry mounting—Bonding paper, cloth, or other artwork to a firm backing (foam core, Plexiglas, substrate) more or less permanently, using adhesives with heat or pressure or both.

dust cover—Kraft paper applied to the back of a frame with adhesive to keep out dust and insects.

filler board—Last piece added into a frame before closing; can be foam core, pH neutral board, mat board, but never regular corrugated board because of acid content. (Acid-free corrugated board is available and suitable for use as filler.)

fillet—Decorative thin strip of wood, often gold or silver, used next to art or between mats.

finishing—Process to give raw wood a protective or decorative coating.

fit—Final step in framing before adding dust cover; to put all the elements into the frame.

floating—Method of displaying art so that all edges are visible.

foam core—Lightweight board; polystyrene sandwiched between two smooth papers; excellent backboard or substrate; available in various thicknesses.

foxing—Patches of dull rust dots probably caused by mildew, mold, or an impurity in the paper or board; accelerated by extreme light and/or moisture or by acid migration from an old mat, or corrugated or wood board backing.

framer's molding—Differs from builder's molding in that it has a built-in rabbet to hold glass and other components from falling through.

Framespace—Commercial product that provides air space between art and glass.

gesso—An all-purpose paint used as a primer on canvas or as a filler. Can be applied thick to form various textures, to repair chipped frames, etc. There are two kinds of gesso: one was originally made from plaster of paris and is used as a base for paintings and gilding; the second is a polymer medium used as a base for finishing and filling frames. The latter one is the gesso referred to in this book.

glass—Available in standard sizes. There are different types: picture glass is thinner, is less likely to have flaws, and is more expensive than single strength glass, which is fine for most work; nonglare, antireflective glass is much more expensive, and diffuses the image in some cases, but is useful in an area where there is a great deal of glare.

glazing—Term used for the glass or Plexiglas that covers artwork.

hinge—A small piece of paper that holds artwork in place; can be made of different materials depending on use, such as Japanese paper, linen tape, pressure-sensitive tape, and a variety of others.

insert—Frame within a frame, often cloth covered.

Japanese hinges—Acid-free paper hinges; strong, thin, and flexible; often made from the bark of Mulberry trees; available in different weights for various size paintings.

joining—Gluing and/or nailing mitered corners to form a frame.

kraft paper—Brown wrapping paper used on back of frames as dust cover.

kerf—Cut made by a saw.

keys—Small pieces of plastic or wood inserted in the corners of canvas stretchers; can be tightened to make canvas taut if it should sag.

liner—An insert between artwork and the frame opening when used with a canvas oil, often cloth covered. The term is also used for a second or third mat when using multiple mats with artwork.

marking gauge—Useful tool for marking out mat sizes.

mat—Protective board around artwork that separates art from glazing and also enhances artwork; window opening generally cut with a bevel.

mat board—Heavy paper board from which mats and backing boards are cut; can be acid-free, 100 percent rag, or "regular." Regular has an acid-free core and backing, but the top colored paper can still be acidic.

mat cutter—Device used to cut windows in mats. There are many different kinds; choice depends upon budget and importance of convenience.

methyl cellulose—Mounting paste with neutral pH made from a powder dissolved in water; exceptionally easy to use; prepared paste has unlimited shelf life.

miter—Joining of two pieces of wood at a corner to form an almost invisible joint.

miter box—Tool with precut guides for sawing molding at exact angles to form a perfect corner; always used with backsaw.

miter vise—Tool for holding two pieces of framing wood, which are being formed into a corner, as glue and brads are applied.

molding—Strips of wood used to make frames.

mount—To secure an object or piece of art to a backboard using adhesive of some type.

mulberry paper—See Japanese paper hinges.

museum board—100 percent rag board used in conservation work.

museum framing—Conservation framing.

nail set—Tool used to countersink nails.

package—Synonymous with assemblage.

parting strip—Wood used with molding to provide rabbet.

pH neutral—Indicates no acidity or alkalinity in a product.

Plexiglas—Lightweight acrylic glazing that is useful for larger pieces of art, especially when shipping; the magnetic attraction makes it unsuitable for use with charcoals or pastels.

rabbet—Area notched into inside edge of wood to hold all the elements that fit into a frame.

rottenstone—A powdery substance with polishing qualities.

spacer—Device used to keep work from touching glazing; can be made of anything convenient, such as strips of balsa wood, mat board, window screen lathing, etc.; available in commercial forms as Innerspace, Framespace, and others.

state of the art—Current level of knowledge of an industry.

strainer—Device to keep frame from bowing; an insert of wood used when outer frame needs reinforcing.

stretcher—Wood frame on which canvas is stretched, with keys used in the inner corners to hold the canvas taut and rectangular.

substrate—Synonymous with backboard.

tack iron—Mounting tool that applies heat in localized spots.

utility knife—Tool with replaceable blade, useful for cutting outsides of mat boards, fabric, and other framing tasks.

window—Opening in a mat through which you view the artwork.

X-Acto knife—Tradename for cutting device, similar to a single-edged razor blade, but has handy grip to make it easier to manipulate.

INDEX

INDEX

187

Other Bestsellers From TAB

☐ **MAJOR HOME APPLIANCES: A Common Sense Repair Manual—Rains**

Prolong the life and efficiency of your major appliances . . . save hundreds of dollars in appliance servicing and repair costs . . . eliminate the inconvenience of having an appliance quit just when you need it most *and* the frustration of having to wait days, even weeks, until you can get a serviceman in to repair it! With the help and advice of service professional Darell L. Rains, even the most inexperienced home handyman can easily keep any major appliances working at top efficiency year after year. 160 pp., 387 illus., Large Format (7″ × 10″).

Paper $14.95   **Hard $21.95**
Book No. 2747

☐ **THE COMPLETE BOOK OF BATHROOMS—Ramsey and Self**

Simple redecorating tricks . . . remodeling advice . . . plumbing techniques . . . it's all here. Find literally hundreds of photographs, drawings, and floorplans to help you decide exactly what kind of remodeling project you'd like to undertake; plus, step-by-step directions for accomplishing your remodeling goals. It's all designed to save you time and money on your bathroom renovations! 368 pp., 474 illus. 7″ × 10″.

Paper $15.95   **Book No. 2708**

☐ **ROOFING THE RIGHT WAY—A Step-By-Step Guide for the Homeowner—Steve Bolt**

If you're faced with having to replace your roof because of hidden leaks, torn or missing shingles, or simply worn roofing that makes your whole house look shabby and run down . . . don't assume that you'll have to take out another mortgage to pay for the project. The fact is, *almost anyone can install a new or replacement roof easily and at amazingly low cost compared with professional contractor prices!* All the professional techniques and step-by-step guidance you'll need is here in this complete new roofing manual written by an experienced roofing contractor. 192 pp., 217 illus. Large Format (7″ × 10″).

Paper $11.95   **Hard $19.95**
Book No. 2667

☐ **PLANNING AND BUILDING FENCES AND GATES**

This colorfully illustrated guide gives you all the expert, step-by-step guidelines and instructions you need to plan and build durable, cost-effective fences and gates. You will be able to design and construct just about any kind of fence you can think of—barbed wire, woven wire, cable wire, mesh wire, board fences, electric fences, gates, and much more! 192 pp., 356 illus. 8 1/2″ × 11″. 2-Color Throughout.

Paper $14.95   **Book No. 2643**

☐ **THE BUILDING PLAN BOOK: Complete Plans for 21 Affordable Homes—Ernie Bryant**

Here, in one impressive, well-illustrated volume, are complete building plans for a total of 21 custom-designed homes offering a full range of styles and features—efficiency dwellings, ranches, capes, two-story homes, split-levels, even duplexes. It's a collection of practical, good looking home designs that not only offer comfort, convenience, and charm but can also be built at a reasonable cost. 352 pp., 316 illus., 8 1/2″ × 11″

Paper $14.95   **Hard $24.95**
Book No. 2714

☐ **THE GARDENING IDEA BOOK**

Whether you have space for a full-space garden or only a pocket size back yard, this exciting collection of articles from *Farmstead Magazine* shows how you can grow all kinds of delicious, healthful fruits and vegetables. Here's expert advice and guidance that's guaranteed to make your garden more productive, easier to take care of, and less expensive! 208 pp., illustrated.

Paper $10.95   **Book No. 2684**

☐ **ALL ABOUT LAMPS; CONSTRUCTION, REPAIR AND RESTORATION—Coggins**

You'll find step-by-step directions for making a wall lamp or a hanging lamp from wood, novelty lamps from PVC plumbing pipe, and designer lamps from acrylic or polyester resins. Shade projects range from needlepoint and fabric models to globes, balls, and tubular forms. There are suggestions for advanced projects, using salvaged and low-cost materials, and more! 192 pp., 196 illus. 7″ × 10″.

Paper $16.95   **Hard $24.95**
Book No. 2658

☐ **101 PROJECTS, PLANS AND IDEAS FOR THE HIGH-TECH HOUSEHOLD**

If you're looking for decorative effects, you'll be impressed with the number of projects that have been included. And electronics hobbyists will be amazed at the array of projects—all of them with clear building instructions, schematics, and construction drawings. You'll also find exciting ways to use your microcomputer as a key decorative element in your high-tech atmosphere. 352 pp., 176 illus. 7″ × 10″.

Paper $16.95   **Book No. 2642**

Other Bestsellers From TAB

☐ **UPHOLSTERY TECHNIQUES ILLUSTRATED —Gheen**

Here's an easy-to-follow, step-by-step guide to modern upholstery techniques that covers everything from stripping off old covers and padding to restoring and installing new foundations, stuffing, cushions, and covers. All the most up-to-date pro techniques are included along with lots of time- and money-saving "tricks-of-the-trade" not usually shared by professional upholsterers. 352 pp., 549 illus., 7″ × 10″.
Paper $16.95   **Book No. 2602**

☐ **CABINETS AND VANITIES—A BUILDER'S HANDBOOK—Godley**

Here in easy-to-follow, step-by-step detail is everything you need to know to design, build, and install your own customized kitchen cabinets and bathroom vanities and cabinets for a fraction of the price charged by professional cabinetmakers or kitchen remodelers . . . and for less than a third of what you'd spend for the most cheaply made, ready-made cabinets and vanities! 142 pp., 126 illus., Paperback
Paper $12.95   **Book No. 1982**

☐ **HARDWOOD FLOORS—INSTALLING, MAINTAINING, AND REPAIRING—Ramsey**

This comprehensive guide includes all the guidance you need to install, restore, maintain, or repair all types of hardwood flooring at costs far below those charged by professional builders and maintenance services. From details on how to select the type of wood floors best suited to your home, to time- and money-saving ways to keep your floors in tip-top condition. 160 pp., 230 illus., 4 pages in full color.
Paper $10.95   **Hard $18.95**
Book No. 1928

☐ **DO YOUR OWN DRYWALL—AN ILLUSTRATED GUIDE**

Proper installation of interior plaster board or drywall is a must-have skill for successful home building or remodeling. Now, there's a new time- and money-saving alternative: this excellent step-by-step guide to achieving professional-quality drywalling results, the first time and *every* time! Even joint finishing, the drywalling step most dreaded by do-it-yourselfers, is a snap when you know what you're doing. 160 pp., 161 illus.
Paper $10.95   **Book No. 1838**

☐ **HOW TO BE YOUR OWN ARCHITECT—2nd Edition—Goddard and Wolverton**

The completely revised version of a long-time bestseller gives you all the expert assistance needed to design your own dream house like a professional. You'll save the money that most custom-home builders put out in architect's fees—an estimated 12% to 15% of the total construction costs—to pay for more of those "extras" you'd like. 288 pp., 369 illus. 7″ × 10″.
Paper $14.95   **Book No. 1790**

☐ **TILE FLOORS—INSTALLING, MAINTAINING AND REPAIRING—Ramsey**

Now you can easily install resilient or traditional hard tiles on both walls and floors. Find out how to buy quality resilient floor products at reasonable cost . . . and discover the types and sizes of hard tiles available. Get step-by-step instructions for laying out the floor, selecting needed tools and adhesives, cutting tiles, applying adhesives, and more. 192 pp., 200 illus., 4 pages in full color. 7″ × 10″.
Paper $12.95   **Hard $22.95**
Book No. 1998

☐ **BUILDING OUTDOOR PLAYTHINGS FOR KIDS, WITH PROJECT PLANS**

Imagine the delight of your youngsters—children or grandchildren—when you build them their own special backyard play area! Best of all, discover how you can make exciting, custom-designed play equipment at a fraction of the cost of ordinary, ready-made swing sets or sandbox units! It's all here in this step-by-step guide to planning and building safe, sturdy outdoor play equipment! 240 pp., 213 illus. 7″ × 10″.
Paper $12.95   **Book No. 1971**

☐ **DO-IT-YOURSELF DESIGNER WINDOWS—Boyle**

If the cost of custom-made draperies puts you in a state of shock . . . if you don't know what to do with a problem window or what type of window decor would look right in your home . . . here's all the advice and information you've been searching for. It's a complete, hands-on guide to selecting, measuring, making, and installing just about any type of window treatment imaginable. 272 pp., 414 illus. 7″ × 10″.
Paper $14.95   **Hard $21.95**
Book No. 1922

☐ **PROFESSIONAL PLUMBING TECHNIQUES— Illustrated and Simplified—Smith**

This plumber's companion includes literally everything about plumbing you'll ever need! From simply changing a washer to installing new fixtures, it covers installing water heaters, water softeners, dishwashers, gas stoves, gas dryers, grease traps, clean outs, and more. Includes piping diagrams, tables, charts, and is arranged alphabetically. 294 pp., 222 illus.
Paper $10.95   **Book No. 1763**

☐ **SUPERINSULATED, TRUSS-FRAME HOUSE CONSTRUCTION**

A revolutionary home building technique that's faster and easier to construct . . . and far less expensive than traditional methods! If you're planning to build or buy a new home . . . or wish you could . . . this book will show you how superinsulated, truss-frame construction can mean having the high-quality, energy-efficient home you want at a fraction of the price you'd expect! 240 pp., 244 illus. 7″ × 10″.
Paper $15.50   **Book No. 1674**

Other Bestsellers From TAB